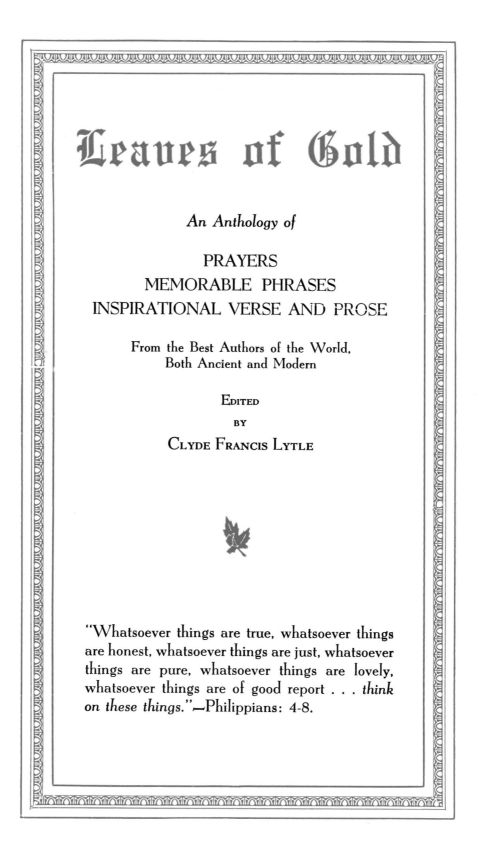

Leaves of Gold

An Anthology of

PRAYERS
MEMORABLE PHRASES
INSPIRATIONAL VERSE AND PROSE

From the Best Authors of the World,
Both Ancient and Modern

EDITED

BY

CLYDE FRANCIS LYTLE

"Whatsoever things are true, whatsoever things
are honest, whatsoever things are just, whatsoever
things are pure, whatsoever things are lovely,
whatsoever things are of good report . . . *think
on these things.*"—Philippians: 4-8.

Published by

THE COSLETT PUBLISHING COMPANY

WILLIAMSPORT, PENNSYLVANIA

PRINTED IN THE UNITED STATES OF AMERICA

Leaves of Gold

Foreword

POOR indeed is the man whose mind is not enriched by some phrase of lasting truth and beauty which serves to restore his soul in the exigencies of life. Each of us needs in his heart's treasury the memory of a lovely line to renew fellowship with the great and noble of this earth—and, indeed, almost as great as the ability to write a line of strength is the ability to use that line to higher levels of emotion and achievement.

To discover afresh in truth expressed with elemental force our eternal kinship with God is a universal urge. "Leaves of Gold" had its origin in the recognition of this impulse. From those who spoke with authority have been chosen words in which the Word becomes flesh to dwell among us. Here are maxims, phrases, anecdotes, passages, proverbs and essays from the best minds among men; here are words of wisdom and thoughts of comfort for all mankind.

Consolation is the objective of "Leaves of Gold"; to provide a key to things of the spirit as inspiration for daily living, its design.

To the great minds, both past and present, who have made the compilation of this volume a pleasant duty, our sincere and humble thanks.—*The Editors.*

Contents

The Heart's Haven

CIVILIZATION had its beginning around an open fire. Here at its warmth gathered the family group to find safety, comfort, and companionship. Trace the origin of our word *fireplace* and you will find it definitely related to the Latin word *focus*. There is the explanation of what home has always meant; for home is the center of life,—no mere residence of the body but the axis of the heart; the place where affections develop themselves, where children love and learn, where two toil together to make life a blessing.

To picture in a word the depths of want, we say of a man that he is homeless. True, life is a journey, and we are all on a pilgrimage. But when distance has lost its enchantment and the ardor for adventure has cooled, when danger has been bravely faced and wonder satiated, hearts long for a resting place and find in the ruddy glows of the hearth-fire "the charm from the skies" that hallows life and gives refuge to man's tired soul.

—THE EDITORS

With unrelenting crescendo, the symphony of a life replete with melodic progression, hastens to its finale. And a friendship that is ours to share, with its "largos" and "allegros" moves ever-lasting; onward, in sweet memories.

I. ACTION

TWO DIVISIONS OF SOCIETY—There are two methods of human activity—and according to which one of these two kinds of activity people mainly follow, are there two kinds of people: one use their reason to learn what is good and what is bad and they act according to this knowledge; the other act as they want to and then they use their reason to prove that that which they did was good and that which they didn't do was bad.—*Leo Tolstoi.*

STANDARD OF JUDGMENT—Men are not to be judged by what they do not know, but by what they know, and by the manner in which they know it.

—*Vauvenargues.*

CHRISTIANITY— is not a voice in the wilderness, but a life in the world. It is not an idea in the air but feet on the ground, going God's way. It is not an exotic to be kept under glass, but a hardy plant to bear twelve months of fruits in all kinds of weather. Fidelity to duty is its root and branch. Nothing we can say to the Lord, no calling Him by great or dear names, can take the place of the plain doing of His will. We may cry out about the beauty of eating bread with Him in His kingdom, but it is wasted breath and a rootless hope, unless we plow and plant in His kingdom here and now. To remember Him at His table and to forget Him at ours, is to have invested in bad securities. There is no substitute for plain, every-day goodness.—*Babcock.*

TWO ALTERNATIVES—We shall meanly lose or nobly save the last hope of earth.—*Abraham Lincoln.*

TRAINING—An athlete was never made by mere instruction. No soldier was ever trained by the mere study of his manual, but by practising his drill. Not the hearers of the law, but the doers are justified before God. We must be going forward, not standing still, simply listening and learning. Where our duty is seen God is revealed. Duty is always the will of God. To see it and not to do it, is a most disastrous thing for the man, as well as being an offense against God.

—*Outlook.*

SERMONS WE SEE

I'd rather see a sermon than hear one
  any day,
I'd rather one should walk with me
  than merely show the way.
The eye's a better pupil and more will-
  ing than the ear;
Fine counsel is confusing, but ex-
  ample's always clear;
And the best of all the preachers are
  the men who live their creeds,
For to see the good in action is what
  everybody needs.
I can soon learn how to do it if you'll
  let me see it done.
I can watch your hands in action, but
  your tongue too fast may run.
And the lectures you deliver may be
  very wise and true;
But I'd rather get my lesson by observ-
  ing what you do.
For I may misunderstand you and the
  high advice you give,
But there's no misunderstanding how
  you act and how you live.

—EDGAR A. GUEST.

"Sermons We See" is from the book "The Light of Faith" by Edgar A. Guest, copyright 1926 by The Reilly & Lee Co., Chicago.

RIGHTEOUSNESS is the fulfillment of God's creative purpose in a man's whole life. It begins with the soul, the real eternal self, that is instinct with the life of the God from whom it came. It is the response of the highest in man to the claim of God.—*Percy C. Ainsworth.*

A Persian Proverb

He who knows not,
And knows not that he knows not,
Is a fool—shun him.
He who knows not,
And knows that he knows not,
Is a child—teach him.
He who knows,
And knows not that he knows,
Is asleep—wake him.
He who knows,
And knows that he knows,
Is wise—follow him.

SUPERFLUITY — True eloquence consists in saying all that is necessary, and nothing but what is necessary.
—*La Rochefoucauld.*

PERSONALITY—It is not what he has, nor even what he does, which directly expresses the worth of a man, but what he is.—*Henri-Frederic Amiel.*

KISMET—I do not believe in a fate that falls on men however they act; but I do believe in a fate that falls on them unless they act.—*G. K. Chesterton.*

DOING VS. DREAMING — Do noble things, not dream them all day long: And so make Life, Death, and the vast Forever one grand, sweet song.
—*Charles Kingsley.*

THE HARVEST—Sow a thought, reap an act; sow an act, reap a habit; sow a habit, reap a character; sow a character, reap a destiny.

WHO LIVES MOST?—We live in deeds, not years; in thoughts, not breaths; in feelings, not in figures on a dial. We should count time by heart-throbs. He most lives who thinks most, feels the noblest, acts the best.
—*Philip James Bailey.*

Worth

It is not what the world gives me
In honor, praise or gold;
It is what I do give the world,
So others do unfold.

If by my work through life I can
Another soul unfold,
Then I have done what cannot be
Made good, by praise or gold.

One tiny thought in tiny word
May give a great one birth,
And, if that thought was caused by me,
I lived a life of worth.
—*Richard F. Wolfe.*

DIVINE SERVICE—Unless we perform divine service with every willing act of our life, we never perform it at all.
—*John Ruskin.*

GROWTH—All growth depends upon activity. There is no development physically or intellectually without effort, and effort means work. Work is not a curse; it is the prerogative of intelligence, the only means to manhood, and the measure of civilization.—*Calvin Coolidge.*

WHAT IS WORTHWHILE?—The world is blessed most by men who do things, and not by those who merely talk about them.—*James Oliver.*

The life of man is made up of action and endurance; the life is fruitful in the ratio in which it is laid out in noble action or in patient perseverance.—*Liddon.*

One thing, and only one, in this world has eternity stamped upon it. Feelings pass; resolves and thoughts pass; opinions change. What you have done lasts—lasts in you. Through ages, through eternity, what you have done for Christ, that, and only that, you are.

—*F. W. Robertson.*

It is well to think well; it is Divine to act well.—*Horace Mann.*

Existence was given us for action, rather than indolent and aimless contemplation; our worth is determined by the good deeds we do, rather than by the fine emotions we feel. They greatly mistake who suppose that God cares for no other pursuit than devotion.—*E. L. Magoon.*

SIN, by its deadly infusions into the soul of man, wastes and eats out the innate vigor of the soul, and casts it into such a deep lethargy, as that it is not able to recover itself.—*J. Smith.*

DISCIPLINE — Thank God every morning when you get up that you have something to do which must be done, whether you like it or not. Being forced to work, and forced to do your best, will breed in you temperance, self-control, diligence, strength of will, content, and a hundred other virtues which the idle never know.—*Charles Kingsley.*

DO SOMETHING—Observe what St. Paul did at Athens. He did something. He was not the man to stand still and "confer with flesh and blood" in the face of a city full of idols. He might have reasoned with himself that he stood alone; that he was a Jew by birth; that he was a stranger in a strange land; that he had to oppose the rooted prejudices and old associations of learned men; that to attack the old religion of a whole city was to beard a lion in his den; that the doctrines of the Gospel were little likely to be effective on minds steeped in Greek philosophy. But none of these thoughts seem to have crossed the mind of St. Paul. He saw souls perishing; he felt that life was short, and time passing away; he had confidence in the power of his Master's message to meet every man's soul; he had received mercy himself, and knew not how to hold his peace. He acted at once, and what his hand found to do he did with all his might. Oh, that we had more men of action in these days!—*Ryle.*

BEST

Like the star,
That shines afar,
Without haste
And without rest,
Let each man wheel with steady sway
Round the task that rules the day,
And do his best.

—*Goethe.*

REALITY—I will be a man among men; and no longer a dreamer among shadows. Henceforth be mine a life of action and reality! I will work in my own sphere, nor wish it other than it is. This alone is health and happiness.

—*Henry W. Longfellow.*

DECISION—The decisive man walks by the light of his own judgment; he has made up his mind; and, having done so, henceforth action is before him. He cannot bear to sit amidst unrealized speculations; to him speculation is only valuable that it may be resolved into living and doing. There is no indifference, no delay. The spirit is in arms: all is in earnest. Thus Pompey, when hazarding his life on a tempestuous sea in order to be at Rome on an important occasion, said, "It is necessary for me to go: it is not necessary for me to live." Thus Caesar, when he crossed the Rubicon, burned the ships upon the shore which brought his soldiers to land, that there might be no return.

—*Paxton Hood.*

THE MINISTER is to be a live man, a real man, a true man, a simple man, great in his love, great in his life, great in his work, great in his simplicity, great in his gentleness.—*John Hall.*

THE PREACHER who deals with the great truths of holy character must impersonate those truths. There is power inherent in truth; but it is often like electricity, needing a conductor to develop it. The preacher who best commends the truth of the gospel to his hearers is he who has translated that truth into his own life, until his life is full of it and redolent of it.—*Anonymous.*

PATIENCE
Let us, then, be up and doing,
With a heart for any fate;
Still achieving, still pursuing,
Learn to labor and to wait.
—*Henry W. Longfellow.*

MASTERPIECES—When love and skill work together expect a masterpiece.
—*Ruskin.*

WHICH ARE YOU?

An attender or an absenter?
A pillar or a sleeper?
A wing or a weight?
A power or a problem?
A promoter or a provoker?
A giver or a getter?
A goer or a gadder?
A doer or a deadhead?
A booter or a bucker?
A supporter or a sponger?
A soldier or a sorehead?
A worker or a worrier?
A friend or a fault-finder?
A helper or a hinderer?
A campaigner or a camper?
—*The Baptist.*

FORTUITOUS—The greatest pleasure I know is to do a good action by stealth and have it found out by accident.
—*Charles Lamb.*

THOUGHT—To act is easy; to think is hard. . .—*Goethe*

DAY DREAMING
I sleep
through my years, in
the shadow of my puny
cosmos, while I should be dusting
the stars.
—*Kermit Oswald.*

GOALS—I find the great thing in this world is, not so much where we stand, as in what direction we are moving.
—*Goethe.*

SCULPTORS—All in their life-time carve their own soul's statue.
—*Thomas Buchanan Read.*

II. ADVERSITY

BURDENS—I compare the troubles which we have to undergo in the course of the year to a great bundle of fagots, far too large for us to lift. But God does not require us to carry the whole at once. He mercifully unties the bundle, and gives us first one stick, which we are to carry today, and then another, which we are to carry tomorrow, and so on. This we might easily manage, if we would only take the burden appointed for us each day; but we choose to increase our troubles by carrying yesterday's stick over again today, and adding tomorrow's burden to our load, before we are required to bear it.—*John Newton.*

SUFFERING — Suffering overcomes the mind's inertia, develops the thinking powers, opens up a new world, and drives the soul to action.—*Anthony H. Evans.*

HIS YOKE IS EASY—A man was carrying a heavy basket. His son asked to help him. The father cut a stick and placed it through the handle of the basket so that the end toward himself was very short, while the end toward the boy was three or four times as long. Each took hold of his end of the stick, and the basket was lifted and easily carried. The son was bearing the burden with the father, but he found his work easy and light because his father assumed the heavy end of the stick. Just so it is when we bear the yoke with Christ; He sees to it that the burden laid on us is light; He carries the heavy end.—*John T. Faris.*

AFFLICTIONS—No affliction would trouble a child of God, if he knew God's reasons for sending it.—*Morgan.*

CARES—Just as there comes a warm sunbeam into every cottage window, so comes a love-beam of God's care and pity for every separate need.

—*Nathaniel Hawthorne.*

SORROW

Go, bury thy sorrow,
  The world hath its share;
Go, bury it deeply,
  Go, hide it with care.
Go, bury thy sorrow,
  Let others be blest;
Go, give them the sunshine,
  And tell God the rest.

OPPORTUNITY

With doubt and dismay you are
  smitten,
You think there's no chance for you,
  son?
Why, the best books haven't been
  written,
The best race hasn't been run,
The best score hasn't been made yet,
The best song hasn't been sung,
The best tune hasn't been played yet;
Cheer up, for the world is young!

No chance? Why, the world is just
  eager
For things that you ought to create.
Its store of true wealth is still meager,
Its needs are incessant and great;
Don't worry and fret, faint hearted,
The chances have just begun.
For the best jobs haven't been started,
The best work hasn't been done.

—BERTON BRALEY.

SPIRITUAL INSIGHT — Illness knocks a lot of nonsense out of us; it induces humility, cuts us down to our own size. It enables us to throw a searchlight upon our inner selves and to discover how often we have rationalized our failures and weaknesses, dodged vital issues and run skulkingly away. For only when the way straitens and the gate grows narrow, do some people discover their soul, their God, or their life work.

Florence Nightingale, too ill to move from her bed, reorganized the hospitals of England. Semi-paralyzed, and under the constant menace of apoplexy, Pasteur was tireless in his attack on disease. The great American historian Francis Parkman is a triumphant prototype of all such conquerors of pain. During the greater part of his life, Parkman suffered so acutely that he could not work for more than five minutes at a time. His eyesight was so wretched that he could scrawl only a few gigantic words on a manuscript, yet he contrived to write nearly 20 magnificent volumes of history.

Even pain confers spiritual insight, a beauty of outlook, a philosophy of life, an understanding and forgiveness of humanity—in short, a quality of peace and serenity—that can scarcely be acquired by the "owner of pure horse flesh." Suffering is a cleansing fire that chars away much of the meanness, triviality and restlessness of so-called "health." Milton declared, "Who best can suffer, best can do." The proof is his *Paradise Lost* written after he was stricken blind.

—Louis E. Bisch.

TROUBLE—Great minds have purposes, others have wishes. Little minds are tamed and subdued by misfortune; but great minds rise above them.

—Washington Irving.

COMFORT OF PURE THOUGHT —The scholar only knows how dear these silent yet eloquent companions of pure thoughts and innocent hours become in the season of adversity. When all that is worldly turns to dross around us, these only retain their steady value. When friends grow cold, and the converse of intimates languishes into vapid civility and commonplace these only continue the unaltered countenance of happier days, and cheer us with that true friendship which never deceived hope nor deserted sorrow.—*Washington Irving.*

Joy Cometh in the Morning

They are not long, the weeping and the laughter,
   Love and desire and hate:
I think they have no portion in us after
   We pass the gate.

They are not long, the days of wine and roses:
   Out of a misty dream
Our path emerges for a while, then closes
   Within a dream.

—Ernest Dowson.

LIFE'S TESTS—The tests of life are to make, not break us. Trouble may demolish a man's business but build up his character. The blow at the outward man may be the greatest blessing to the inner man. If God, then, puts or permits anything hard in our lives, be sure that the real peril, the real trouble, is that we shall lose if we flinch or rebel.

—M. D. Babcock.

DIFFICULTIES—Life is always difficult in proportion to its intensity and reality.—*Edward Howard Griggs.*

EVEN THIS SHALL PASS AWAY

Once in Persia reigned a King
Who upon his signet ring
Graved a maxim true and wise,
Which, if held before the eyes,
Gave him counsel at a glance,
Fit for every change and chance.
Solemn words, and these are they:
"Even this shall pass away."

Trains of camels through the sand
Brought his gems from Samarcand;
Fleets of galleys through the seas
Brought him pearls to match with these.
But he counted not his gain
Treasures of the mine or main;
"What is wealth?" the king would say;
"Even this shall pass away."

In the revels of his court
At the zenith of the sport,
When the palms of all his guests
Burned with clapping at his jests;
He amid his figs and wine,
Cried: "Oh loving friends of mine!
Pleasure comes but not to stay;
Even this shall pass away."

Fighting on a furious field,
Once a javelin pierced his shield;
Soldiers with a loud lament
Bore him bleeding to his tent;
Groaning from his tortured side,
"Pain is hard to bear," he cried,
"But with patience, day by day,—
Even this shall pass away."

Towering in the public square,
Twenty cubits in the air,
Rose his statue, carved in stone,
Then, the king, disguised, unknown,
Stood before his sculptured name
Musing meekly, "What is fame?
Fame is but a slow decay—
Even this shall pass away."

Struck with palsy, sere and old,
Waiting at the gates of gold,
Said he with his dying breath;
"Life is done, but what is death?"
Then, in answer to the King,
Fell a sunbeam on his ring,
Showing by a heavenly ray,
"Even this shall pass away."
                              —*Theodore Tilton.*

CROSS—In the cross of Christ we glory, because we regard it as a matchless exhibition of the attributes of God. We see there the love of God, desiring a way by which He might save mankind, aided by His wisdom, so that a plan is perfected by which the deed can be done without violation of truth and justice. In the cross we see a strange conjunction of what once appeared to be two opposite qualities— justice and mercy. We see how God is supremely just; as just as if He had no mercy, and yet infinitely merciful in the gift of His Son. Mercy and justice, in fact, become counsel upon the same side, and irresistibly plead for the acquittal of the believing sinner. We can never tell which of the attributes of God shines most glorious in the sacrifice of Christ; they each one find a glorious high throne in the person and work of the Lamb of God, that taketh away the sin of the world. Since it has become, as it were, the disc which reflects the character and perfections of God, it is meet that we should glory in the cross of Christ, and none shall stay us of our boasting.—*Spurgeon.*

BROKEN HOPES—As the tree is fertilized by its own broken branches and fallen leaves, and grows out of its own decay, so men and nations are bettered and improved by trial, and refined out of broken hopes and blighted expectations.
                              —*F. W. Robertson.*

SPIRITUAL RESOURCES — The man who has no refuge in himself, who lives, so to speak, in his front rooms, in the outer whirlwind of things and opinions, is not properly a personality at all.

He floats with the current, who does not guide himself according to higher principles, who has no ideal, no convictions—such a man is a mere article of the world's furniture—a thing moved, instead of a living and moving being—an echo, not a voice. The man who has no inner life is the slave of his surroundings, as the barometer is the obedient servant of the air at rest, and the weathercock the humble servant of the air in motion.

—*Henri-Frederic Amiel.*

Tears

When I consider life and its few years—
A wisp of fog betwixt us and the sun;
A call to battle and the battle done
Ere the last echo dies within our ears;
A rose choked in the grass; an hour of
    fears;
The gusts that past a darkening shore
    do beat;
A burst of music down an unlistening
    street—
I wonder at the idleness of tears.
Ye, old, old dead, and ye of yesternight,
Chieftains and bards and keepers of the
    sheep:
By every cup of sorrow that you had,
Loose me from tears, and make me see
    aright
How each hath back what once he stayed
    to weep;
Homer his sight, David his little lad!
    —*Lizette Woodworth Reese.*

HUMILITY—One of the great lessons seldom effectively taught in college is the lesson of humility. It is usually the first of a long series of lessons we learn in our postgraduate course, when "the cold, cold world" is our instructor. This was subtly suggested in a cartoon appearing once in a New York paper late in June. It pictured a young woman in cap and gown, armed with her college diploma and a sufficient amount of self-satisfied dignity. Confronting her was the grim visage of the old World himself, who remarked rather casually, "Well, who have we here?" "You evidently don't know me," replied the slightly pained young graduate; "I am Virginia Cordelia Smith, A.B." "My dear girl," replied the World, "come with me and I will teach you the rest of your alphabet."—*George Walter Fiske.*

COMPLAINT — Impatient people water their miseries and hoe up their comforts; sorrows are visitors that come without invitation, and complaining minds send a wagon to bring their troubles home in.—*C. H. Spurgeon.*

FAILURE—There are few positions in life in which difficulties have not to be encountered. These difficulties are, however, our best instructors, as our mistakes often form our best experience. We learn wisdom from failure more than from success. We often discover what will do by finding out what will not do. Horne Tooke used to say that he had become all the better acquainted with the country from having had the good luck sometimes to lose his way. Great thoughts, discoveries, inventions have very generally been nurtured in hardship, often pondered over in sorrow and established with difficulty.
—*Paxton Hood.*

OUT OF GREAT TRIBULATION

—No words can express how much the world owes to sorrow. Most of the Psalms were born in a wilderness. Most of the Epistles were written in a prison. The greatest thoughts of the greatest thinkers have all passed through fire. The greatest poets have "learned in suffering what they taught in song." In bonds Bunyan lived the allegory that he afterwards indited, and we may thank Bedford Jail for the "Pilgrim's Progress." Take comfort, afflicted Christian! When God is about to make pre-eminent use of a man, He puts him in the fire.—*Macdonald.*

BURDENS—We have all of us sufficient fortitude to bear the misfortunes of others.—*La Rochefoucauld.*

STRENGTH—We never have more than we can bear. The present hour we are always able to endure. As our day, so is our strength. If the trials of many years were gathered into one, they would overwhelm us; therefore, in pity to our little strength, He sends first one, and then another, then removes both, and lays on a third, heavier, perhaps, than either; but all is so wisely measured to our strength that the bruised reed is never broken. We do not enough look at our trials in this continuous and successive view. Each one is sent to teach us something, and altogether they have a lesson which is beyond the power of any to teach alone.—*H. E. Manning.*

MISFORTUNE—It requires greater virtues to support good fortune than bad.
—*La Rochefoucauld*

LIFE is a long lesson in humility.
—*James M. Barrie.*

THE ROSARY OF MY TEARS

Some reckon their age by years,
    Some measure their life by art;
But some tell their days by the flow of
        their tears,
    And their lives by the moans of their
        heart.

The dials of earth may show
    The length, not the depth of years,
Few or many they come, few or many
        they go,
    But time is best measured by tears.

For the young are oft-times old,
    Though their brows be bright and fair;
While their blood beats warm, their
        hearts are cold,
    O'er them the spring—but winter is
        there.

And the old are oft-times young,
    When their hair is thin and white;
And they sing in age, as in youth they
        sung,
    And they laugh for their cross was light.

But, bead by bead, I tell
    The rosary of my years,
From a cross to a cross they lead; 'tis well
    And they're blest with a blessing of
        tears.

Better a day of strife
    Than a century of sleep;
Give me instead of a long stream of life
    The tempests and tears of the deep.

A thousand joys may foam
    On the billows of all the years;
But never the foam brings the lone back
        home;
    It reaches the haven through tears.
        —*Abram J. Ryan.*

III. AGE

REVALUATION—Age, that lessens the enjoyment of life, increases our desire of living. Those dangers which, in the vigor of youth, we had learned to despise, assume new terrors as we grow old. Our caution increasing as our years increase, fear becomes at last the prevailing passion of the mind, and the small remainder of life is taken up in useless efforts to keep off our end, or provide for a continued existence. Whence, then, is this increased love of life, which grows upon us with our years? Whence comes it that we thus make greater efforts to preserve our existence at a period when it becomes scarce worth the keeping? Is it that Nature, attentive to the preservation of mankind, increases our wishes to live, while she lessens our enjoyments; and, as she robs the senses of every pleasure, equips imagination in the spoil? Life would be insupportable to an old man, who loaded with infirmities, feared death no more than when in the vigor of manhood: the numberless calamities of decaying Nature, and the consciousness of surviving every pleasure would at once induce him with his own hand to terminate the scene of misery: but happily the contempt of death forsakes him at a time when it could only be prejudicial, and life acquires an imaginary value in proportion as its real value is no more.—*Oliver Goldsmith.*

"THALATTA"

I stand upon the summit of my years.
Behind, the toil, the camp, the march,
*   the strife,*
The wandering and the desert; vast,
*   afar,*
Beyond this weary way, behold! the
*   Sea!*
The sea o'erswept by clouds and winds
*   and wings,*
By thoughts and wishes manifold,
*   whose breath*
Is freshness and whose mighty pulse is
*   peace.*
Palter no question of the dim Beyond;
Cut lose the bark; such voyage itself
*   is rest;*
Majestic motion, unimpeded scope,
A widening heaven, a current without
*   care.*
Eternity!   Deliverance,   Promise,
*   Course!*
Time-tired souls salute thee from the
*   shore.*

—J. B. BROWN.

THE PRELUDES—Winter is on my head, but eternal spring is in my heart; I breathe at this hour the fragrance of the lilacs, the violets, and the roses, as at twenty years ago. The nearer I approach to the end, the plainer I hear around me the immortal symphonies of the worlds which invite me.—*Victor Hugo.*

REST

Rest is not quitting
    The busy career;
Rest is the fitting
    Of self to its sphere.
'Tis loving and serving
    The highest and best!
'Tis onwards, unswerving,
    And that is true rest.
                    —*J. S. Dwight.*

QUIET MINDS can not be perplexed or frightened, but go on in fortune or misfortune at their own private pace, like a clock during a thunderstorm.
                    —*Robert Louis Stevenson.*

FOOTFALLS—Yes, we are all growing old, though unconsciously, and the foot of time falls as softly as ever, and the current of life flows on as smoothly as ever—indeed, the fuller the current, the more noiseless its flow. And months and years are, after all, so very much alike that they pass away without special observation, and we begin to get old before we think of it. And when we sit down to a simple sum in arithmetic—the subtraction of the year of our birth from the current year—we are astonished at the answer, and are so doubtful of its correctness that we go over it a second time, but always with the same result. Children grow up around us, but we get used to that, and are so busy that we seldom stop to compute their ages and realize the swift flight of the years. In fact, our children never get old to us. The wife who has stood lovingly and faithfully at our side so long, never changes, and is always the fair young bride of the old and happy days. Though his hair may have grown grey in some way which we do not exactly understand, and his step may seem a little less elastic, and firm than it was, the husband does not seem to have changed much, after all—*Balfern.*

BETTER THAN SERMONS — I think that to have known one good, old man—one man, who, through the chances and mischances of a long life, has carried his heart in his hand, like a palm-branch, waving all discords into peace—helps our faith in God, in ourselves, and in each other more than many sermons.
—*G. W. Curtis.*

THE GREATEST SIN—Stanley Hall once called the great sin of maturity losing one's zest for life.

TRUTH—Did you ever see a man sitting in his own orchard with the trees (which he planted with his own hand) pouring down their ripened fruit upon him, and he and his children and his grandchildren rejoicing in its beauty? That is the picture of a man who took the truth and planted it, and now he is sitting under the boughs that overarch him. His days are happy and his life is full of joy and usefulness.

EVENTIDE

God loves the Aged.
He gives them greater visions than the young;
He puts the words of wisdom on their tongue;
And keeps His presence ever by their side,
From dawn to dusk. and on through eventide.

God helps the Aged.
Within their home His Spirit ever dwells;
Their mellow hearts are touched like chiming bells;
He calms their fears, then worries disappear,
Because they know His help is always near.

God keeps the Aged.
With hearts of gold, and silver-tinted hair,
And earnestness, and greater faith in prayer;
He keeps them as a shepherd guards his sheep,
'Til in His fold they gently fall asleep.
—*Charles W. H. Bancroft.*

BIRTHDAYS—Forty is the old age of youth; fifty is the youth of old age.
—*Victor Hugo.*

SUCCESS—That you may find success, let me tell you how to proceed. Tonight begin your great plan of life. You have but one life to live; yet it is most important that you should not make a mistake. Tonight begin carefully. Fix your eye on the fortieth year of your age, and then say to yourself, "At the age of forty, I will be an industrious man, a benevolent man, a well-read man, a religious man, and a useful man; I resolve and will stand to it."

—C. Brooks.

When You Are Old

When you are old and gray and full of
    sleep,
And nodding by the fire, take down this
    book,
And slowly read and dream of the soft
    look
Your eyes had once, and of their shadows
    deep;

How many loved your moments of glad
    grace,
And loved your beauty with love false or
    true;
But one man loved the pilgrim soul in you,
And loved the sorrows of your changing
    face.

And bending down beside the glowing
    bars
Murmur, a little sadly, how love fled
And paced upon the mountains overhead
And hid his face amid a crowd of stars.

—William Butler Yeats.

From COLLECTED POEMS of William Butler Yeats.
By permission of The Macmillan Company, publishers; The
Macmillan Company of Canada; and A. P. Watts & Co.,
London.

PERSPECTIVE—To be seventy years young is sometimes far more cheerful and hopeful than to be forty years old.

—Oliver Wendell Holmes.

DIVINE DISCONTENT—Growth is gladdening. He who grows in holiness grows in joy. Spiritual strength brings gladness. It is a poor, half-hearted religion—not spiritual power, but the want of it—that breeds gloom. The consciousness that a man is becoming stronger in his faith, clearer in his convictions, warmer in his love, must, from its very nature, be a glad consciousness. And the hope of greater strength yet to be attained, of loftier heights yet to be reached, is more joyous still. A story is told of Torwaldsen, the sculptor, that on one occasion, when he was adding a few finishing touches to one of his masterpieces—a statue of Christ—a friend called upon him at his studio, and found him in a very depressed and despondent mood. On inquiring the cause of this unusual and apparently untimely depression, the sculptor gave this singular answer—pointing to his work, he said, "I can see no fault in it; my genius is decaying; it is the first of my works that I have felt satisfied with."—Messenger.

HEALTH—It is a sum of money in the bank, which will support you, economically spent. But you spend foolishly and draw on the principal. This diminishes the income, and you draw larger and larger drafts until you become bankrupt. Overeating, overworking, every imprudence is a draft on life which health cashes and charges at a thousand per cent interest. Every abuse of health hastens death!—F. G. Welch.

Serenity

And so, beside the silent sea,
    I wait the muffled oar;
No harm from Him can come to me
    On ocean or on shore.

—John Greenleaf Whittier.

GOODNESS — If you would keep young and happy, be good; live a high moral life; practice the principles of the brotherhood of man; send out good thoughts to all, and think evil of no man. This is in obedience to the great natural law; to live otherwise is to break this great Divine law. Other things being equal, it is the cleanest, purest minds that live long and are happy. The man who is growing and developing intellectually does not grow old like the man who has stopped advancing, but when ambition, aspirations and ideals halt, old age begins.—*Public Speakers Library.*

YOUTH — It is refreshing to find a clergyman willing to defend the youth of today. Unfortunately the defense of the youth of today is too frequently made by lawyers.—*Crane.*

THE THRESHOLD

The seas are quiet when the winds give
    o'er;
So calm are we when passions are no
    more.
For then we know how vain it was to
    boast
Of fleeting things, so certain to be lost.
Clouds of affection from our younger eyes
Conceal that emptiness which age des-
    cries.

The soul's dark cottage, batter'd and
    decay'd,
Lets in new light through chinks that
    Time hath made:
Stronger by weakness, wiser men become
As they draw near to their eternal home.
Loving the old, both worlds at once they
    view
That stand upon the threshold of the new.
    —*Edmund Waller.*

TIME—The days of the years of our pilgrimage are threescore years and ten. The generations crowd each other off the stage of time in swift succession. The sand runs out in the hour glass. Time is only the tick of the second hand in the clock of the ages. Some morning the senses will fail to resume business. Every door will be locked, every shutter drawn. Eye, ear, and hand will fail to respond. There will no longer be any medium by which to enter the temporal. An invisible hand has written "finis" across another human career, and people say "the man is dead." He has not ceased to be; he has merely finished with time.
    —*Anonymous.*

NEARER HOME—An aged Christian, with the snow of time on his head, may remind us that those points of earth are whitest which are nearest Heaven.
    —*Chapin.*

ASHES AND FLAMES—Oftentimes we look with forebodings to the time of old age, forgetful that at eventide it shall be light. To many saints of old age it is the choicest season in their lives. A balmier air fans the mariner's cheek as he nears the shore of immortality; fewer waves ruffle his sea, quiet reigns, deep, still, and solemn. From the altar of age the ashes of the fire of youth are gone, but the flame of more earnest feeling remains.
    —*Selected.*

BRINGING UP FATHER—When I was a boy of 14, my father was so ignorant I could hardly stand to have the old man around. But when I got to be 21, I was astonished at how much the old man had learned in seven years.
    —*Mark Twain.*

IV. ANALOGIES

LIKE FLAKES of snow that fall imperceptibly upon the earth, the seeming unimportant events of life succeed one another.—As the snowflakes gather, so our *habits* are formed.—No single flake that is added to the pile produces a sensible change—No single action creates, however it may exhibit, a man's character.—But as the tempest hurls the avalanche down the mountain and overwhelms the inhabitant and his habitation, so *passion*, acting on the elements of mischief which pernicious habits have brought together, may overthrow the edifice of truth and virtue.—*Bentham.*

GRAY HAIRS—seem to my fancy like the soft light of the moon, silvering over the evening of life.—*Richter.*

Enthusiasm is reason gone mad to achieve a definite, rational objective.

Enthusiasm is inflamed by opposition, but never converted; it is the leaping lighting that blasts obstacles from its path.

Enthusiasm is the X-ray of the soul, that penetrates and reveals the invisible.

Enthusiasm is a contagion that laughs at quarantine and inoculates all who come in contact with it.

Enthusiasm is the vibrant thrill in your voice that sways the wills of others into harmony with your own.

Enthusiasm is the "philosopher's stone" that transmutes dull tasks into delightful deeds.

Enthusiasm is a magnet that draws kindred souls with irresistible force and electrifies them with the magnetism of its own resolves.

—PRESBYTERIAN OF THE SOUTH.

DIFFICULTY is the nurse of *greatness*—a harsh nurse, who rocks her foster children roughly, but rocks them into strength and athletic proportions.—The mind, grappling with great aims and wrestling with mighty impediments, grows by a certain necessity to the stature of greatness—*Bryant.*

THE LOSS OF A FRIEND is like that of a limb; time may heal the anguish of the wound, but the loss cannot be repaired.—*Southey.*

THE SERMON OF LIFE—Our birth is the text. Youth the introduction. During manhood we lay down a few propositions and prove them. Some passages are dull and some sprightly. Then come Inferences and Application. At seventy we say, "Fifthly and lastly." The Doxology is sung. The Benediction is pronounced. The book is closed. It is getting cold. Frost on the window pane. Audience gone. Shut up the church. Sexton goes home with the key on his shoulder—*Talmage.*

HAPPINESS is like manna; it is to be gathered in grains, and enjoyed every day. It will not keep; it cannot be accumulated; nor have we got to go out of ourselves or into remote places to gather it, since it is rained down from Heaven, at our very doors.—*Tryon Edwards.*

FALSE HAPPINESS is like false money; it passes for a time as well as the true, and serves some ordinary occasions; but when it is brought to the touch, we find the lightness and alloy, and feel the loss.—*Pope.*

LIFE is like a beautiful and winding lane, on either side bright flowers, beautiful butterflies, and tempting fruits, which we scarcely pause to admire and taste, so eager are we to hasten to an opening which we imagine will be more beautiful still. But by degrees, as we advance, the trees grow bleak, the flowers and butterflies fail, the fruits disappear, and we find that we have arrived—to reach a desert waste.—*Sala.*

TROUBLES—I think that human life is much like road life. You stand on a hill, and look down and across the valley, and another prodigious hill lifts itself upon the other side. The day is hot, your horse is weary, and you are tired; and it seems to you that you cannot climb that long hill. But you had better trot down the hill you are on, and not trouble yourself about the other one. You find the valley pleasant and inspiring. When you get across it, you meet only a slight ascent, and begin to wonder where the steep hill is which your saw. You drive along briskly, and when you reach the highest point, you find that there has not been an inch of the hill over which you have not trotted. You see that it was illusory. The slight ascent looked almost like a perpendicular steep; but when you come to pass over it, step by step, you find it to be a good traveling road.

So it is with your troubles. Just in that way your anticipations of mischief hang before you; and when you come to where they are, you find them to be all smooth turnpikes. Men ought to be ashamed, after they have done that two or three times, not to take the hint, and profit by it; yet they will not. They will suffer from anticipated troubles just as much as though they had no such experience. They have not wit enough to make use of the lesson which their life is continually teaching them;

namely, that a large majority of the troubles which they worry themselves about beforehand either never come or are easily borne. They form a habit of fretting about future troubles. It was not the old monks alone who wore sackcloth and hair shirts; you wear them as much as they did; only you wear them inside, while they wore them outside—you wear them in your heart, they wore them on their skins. They were wiser than you are.—*Beecher.*

DESPAIR is like forward children, who, when you take away one of their playthings, throw the rest into the fire for madness. It grows angry with itself, turns its own executioner, and revenges its misfortunes on its own head—*Charron.*

HAPPINESS is as a butterfly, which, when pursued, is always beyond our grasp, but which, if you will sit down quietly, may alight upon you.
—*Hawthorne.*

OUR DEEDS are seeds of fate, sown here on earth, but bringing forth their harvest in eternity.—*Boardman.*

REVERENCE—It is with men as with wheat; the light heads are erect even in the presence of Omnipotence, but the full heads bow in reverence before Him.
—*Cooke.*

GENIUS is the gold in the mine; talent is the miner who works and brings it out.
—*Lady Blessington.*

GOSSIP, pretending to have the eyes of Argus, has all the blindness of a bat.
—*Ouida.*

PALM TREE—The Scripture says: "The righteous shall flourish like the palm tree." Let us see what this comparison means: "The palm grows not in the depths of the forest or in a fertile loam, but in the desert. Its verdure often springs apparently from the scorching dust. 'It is a friendly lighthouse, guiding the traveler to the spot where water is to be found.'" The tree is remarkable for its beauty, its erect aspiring growth, its leafy canopy, its waving plumes, the emblem of praise in all ages. Its very foliage is the symbol of joy and exultation. It never fades, and the dust never settles upon it. It was, therefore, twisted into the booths of the feasts of tabernacles, was borne aloft by the multitude that accompanied the Messiah to Jerusalem, and it is represented as in the hands of the redeemed in Heaven. For usefulness, the tree is unrivalled. Gibbon says that the natives of Syria speak of 360 uses to which the palm is applied. Its shade refreshes the traveler. Its fruit restores his strength. When his soul fails for thirst, it announces water. Its stones are ground for his camels. Its leaves are made into couches, its boughs into fences and walls, and its fibres into ropes or rigging. Its best fruit, moreover, is borne in old age; the finest dates being often gathered when the tree has reached a hundred years. It sends, too, from the same root a large number of suckers, which in time, form a forest by their growth. What an emblem of the righteous in the desert of a guilty world!—*Joseph Angus.*

THE ACTIONS of men are like the index of a book; they point out what is most remarkable in them.—*Heine.*

BEAUTY is like an almanac: if it lasts a year it is well.—*T. Adams.*

HAPPINESS is a sunbeam which may pass through a thousand bosoms without losing a particle of its original ray; nay, when it strikes a kindred heart, like the converged light upon a mirror, it reflects itself with redoubled brightness.—It is not perfected till it is shared.—*Jane Porter.*

WISE ANGER is like the fire from the flint; there is a great ado to bring it out; and when it does come, it is out again immediately.—*M. Henry.*

LIFE, like war, is a series of mistakes, and he is not the best Christian nor the best general who makes the fewest mistakes. Poor mediocrity may secure that, but he is best who wins the most splendid victories by the retrieval of mistakes.
—*Robertson.*

HOPE is like the sun, which, as we journey toward it, casts the shadow of our burden behind us.—*S. Smiles.*

THE LIGHT of *friendship* is like the light of phosphorus, seen plainest when all around it is dark.—*Crowell.*

DEATH is the golden key that opens the palace of eternity.—*Milton.*

MARRIAGE resembles a pair of shears, so joined that they cannot be separated, often moving in opposite directions, yet always punishing anyone who comes between them.—*Sydney Smith.*

REASON clears and plants the wilderness of the imagination to harvest the wheat of art.—*Austin O'Malley.*

THE EVERYDAY CARES and duties, which men call drudgery, are the weights and counterpoises of the clock of time, giving its pendulum a true vibration, and its hands a regular motion; and when they cease to hang upon the wheels, the pendulum no longer swings, the hands no longer move, and the clock stands still.
—*Longfellow.*

NATURE is the glass reflecting God, as by the sea reflected is the sun, too glorious to be gazed on in his sphere.
—*Young.*

MARRIAGE is the Keeley cure for love's intoxication.—*Helen Rowland.*

HOPE is like the cork to a net, which keeps the soul from sinking in despair; and *fear*, like the lead in the net, which keeps it from floating in presumption.
—*Watson.*

A BOOK may be compared to your neighbor: if it be good, it cannot last too long; if bad, you cannot get rid of it too early.—*Brooke.*

NATURE is an Aeolian harp, a musical instrument, whose tones are the re-echo of the higher strings within us.—*Novalis.*

FALSE FRIENDSHIP, like the ivy, decays and ruins the wall it embraces; but *true friendship* gives new life and animation to the object it supports.—*Burton.*

MEN'S FAME is like their hair, which grows after they are dead, and with just as little use to them.—*Villiers.*

SPIRIT—The new position of the Christian is like that of a bankrupt, for whom his liabilities have been met, and who is set up with a new capital, in a new partnership, to make a new start in a new world. God interests Himself for His client's future righteousness. God frees him from the obligations of the past that he may henceforth labor, unencumbered with any liabilities, at this righteousness. God supplies power for this righteousness by a special grant of His own spirit from Himself.—*T. Griffith.*

OVID FINELY compares a broken *fortune* to a falling column; the lower it sinks, the greater the weight it is obliged to sustain.—*Goldsmith.*

THE MARRIED MAN is like the bee that fixes his hive, augments the world, benefits the republic, and by daily diligence, without wronging any, profits all; but he who contemns wedlock, like a wasp, wanders an offense in the world, lives upon spoil, disturbs peace, steals sweets that are none of his own, and meets misery as his just reward.—*Feltham.*

THE AVARICIOUS man is like the barren sandy ground of the desert which sucks in all the rain and dew with greediness, but yields no fruitful herbs or plants for the benefit of others.—*Zeno.*

DEATH is like thunder in two particulars: we are alarmed at the sound of it, and it is formidable only from that which has preceded it.—*Colton.*

A NOBLE DEED is a step toward God.—*Holland.*

DIVINE FIRE—Look at a coal covered with ashes; there is nothing appearing in the hearth but only dead ashes; there is neither light, nor smoke, nor heat; and yet when these embers are stirred to the bottom, there are found some living gleams, which do but contain fire, and are apt to propagate it. Many a Christian breast is like this hearth, no life of grace appearing there for the time, either to his own sense or to the apprehension of others. Whilst the season of temptation lasteth, all seems cold and dead; yet still at the worst there is a secret coal in his bosom, which, upon the gracious motion of the Almighty, doth manifest some remainders of that Divine fire, as is easily raised to a perfect flame. Let no man, therefore, deject himself, or censure others, for the utter extinction of that spirit which doth but hide itself in the soul for a glorious advantage.—*Spencer.*

LEARNING is like mercury, one of the most powerful and excellent things in the world in skillful hands; in the unskillful, the most mischievous.—*Pope.*

LIFE, like a dome of many-colored glass, stains the white radiance of eternity.—*Shelley.*

CLEAR WRITERS, like clear fountains, do not seem so deep as they are; the turbid look the most profound.
—*Landor.*

PITHY SENTENCES are like sharp nails which force truth upon our memory.
—*Diderot.*

JOYS are our wings; sorrows our spurs.
—*Richter.*

MINISTERS should not be merely like dials on watches, or milestones on the road, but like clocks and sirens, to sound the alarm to sinners. Aaron wore bells as well as pomegranates, and the prophets were commanded to lift up their voices like a trumpet. A sleeping sentinel may be the loss of the city.—*Joseph Hall.*

AS WINTER strips the leaves from around us, so that we may see the distant regions they formerly concealed, so *old age* takes away our enjoyments only to enlarge the prospect of the coming eternity.—*Richter.*

DOUBT is the vestibule which all must pass before they can enter the temple of wisdom.—*Colton.*

IT IS of *eloquence* as of a flame; it requires matter to feed it, and motion to excite it; and it brightens as it burns.
—*Tacitus.*

HUMILITY—Trees that, like the poplar, lift upward all their boughs, give no shade and shelter whatever their height. Trees the most lovingly shelter and shade us when, like the willow, the higher soar their summits, the lowlier droop their boughs.—*Bulwer.*

AN UNGRATEFUL MAN is like a hog under a tree eating acorns, but never looking up to see where they come from.
—*Timothy Dexter.*

FALSE FRIENDS are like our shadow, keeping close to us when we walk in the sunshine, but leaving us the instant we cross into the shade.—*Bovee.*

HE WHO does a kindness to an *ungrateful* person, sets his seal to a flint and sows his seed upon sand; on the former he makes no impression, and from the latter finds no product.—*South.*

TEARS are the safety valve of the heart when too much pressure is laid on it.—*Albert Smith.*

LIKE the bee, we should make our *industry* our amusement.—*Goldsmith.*

AN UNJUST ACCUSATION is like a barbed arrow, which must be drawn backward with horrible anguish, or else it will be your destruction.
—*Jeremy Taylor.*

LEISURE is a beautiful garment, but it will not do for constant wear.—*Anon.*

LEARNING, like money, may be so base a coin as to be utterly void of use; or, if sterling, may require good management to make it serve the purposes of sense or happiness.—*Shenstone.*

LIFE is like music; it must be composed by ear, feeling, and instinct, not by rule.—*Samuel Butler.*

JEALOUSY is like a polished glass held to the lips when life is in doubt; if there be breath it will catch the damp and show it.—*Dryden.*

THE SORROWS of a noble soul are as May frosts, which precede the milder season; but the sorrows of a hardened, lost soul are as autumn frosts, which foretell but the coming of winter.—*Richter.*

SORROW is our John the Baptist, clad in grim garments, with rough arms, a son of the wilderness, baptizing us with bitter tears, preaching repentance; and behind him comes the gracious, affectionate, healing Lord, speaking peace and joy to the soul.—*Huntington.*

A PRINTED SPEECH is like a dried flower: the substance indeed is there, but the color is faded and the perfume gone.
—*Lorain.*

UNITY—In a mighty auditorium are four men. They really desire to come together, but neither will come to another's corner. In the center of the room is a beautiful fountain. Finally someone proposes that they all meet at the fountain. They start for the common center. They come on —forty—fifty—one hundred feet. The nearer they come to the fountain, the nearer they come to each other, each making concessions of location and space. At last they reach their destination, and clasp hands around the sparkling waters of the fountain. Jesus Christ, the great fountain of life, liberty and love, is set up in the center of the world. The nearer God's children come to Christ, the nearer they will come to each other. Let us help hasten the day when we can all clasp hands and sing, "Blest be the tie that binds our hearts in Christian love." Let the Christian world strike hands in the spirit of those of old, who said, "We are brethren."—*Hall.*

STYLE is the gossamer on which the seeds of truth float through the world.
—*Bancroft.*

TIME is the chrysalis of eternity.
—*Richter.*

COMPARISONS.—Robert Hall once told a minister that the chief fault he found with his sermons was that there were no "likes" in them. He didn't like them on that account. I must say I shouldn't care to live in a house that was all windows, yet I fancy it would be rather dull and dingy in a house that hadn't any. An occasional opening relieves the deadness of the brick wall. So Christ's utterances were lit up with frequent "likes" of all kinds, and the "common people" were charmed with them, and liked them uncommonly.

Benjamin Franklin, the distinguished natural philosopher, made known to the world some of his important discoveries in regard to lightning and electricity by means of such a paltry instrument as a child's kite. So the Great Teacher that came from God brought the most exalted truths down to the level of the humblest understanding, and that through the use of comparisons and illustrations the most simple and plain possible. He took them all from every-day life. He used to talk to farmers about corn and mustard, wheat and tares, sheep and goats, and such like matters, all purely agricultural, and which they thoroughly understood. He used to talk to fishermen about matters widely different, and such as belonged to their craft—nets and fishes; to gardeners about vines and fig-trees; to women about domestic matters, such as come within their province—kneading dough and sweeping houses. By means of these familiar figures He teaches lessons unheard-of before—lessons of Divine wisdom, of supreme value, of sweet interest, of infinite love, and of eternal importance.—*Thomas.*

TEMPTATION is the fire that brings up the scum of the heart.—*Boston.*

PRIDE, like laudanum and other poisonous medicines, is beneficial in small, though injurious in large, quantities. No man who is not pleased with himself, even in a personal sense, can please others.
—*Frederick Saunders*

KNOWLEDGE is not a couch whereon to rest a searching and restless spirit; nor a terrace for a wandering mind to walk upon with a fair prospect; nor a tower of state for a proud mind to raise itself upon; nor a sort of commanding ground for strife and contention; nor a shop for profit and sale; but a rich storehouse for the glory of the Creator, and the relief of man's estate.—*Bacon.*

PRAISE—No ashes burn lighter than those of incense, and few things burn out sooner.—*Landor.*

OH! TO BE CLEAN as a mountain river! Clean as the air above the clouds, or on the middle seas! As the throbbing ether that fills the gulf between star and star! Nay, as the thought of the Son of Man Himself.—*George Macdonald.*

SUNDAY is the golden clasp that binds together the volume of the week.
—*Longfellow.*

PRIDE, like a magnet, constantly points to one object, self; unlike the magnet, it has no attractive pole, but at all points repels.—*Colton.*

CHURCH—The church is not a dormitory for sleepers, it is an institution for workers; it is not a rest camp, it is a front line trench.—*Sunday.*

CHRISTIANS are like the several flowers in a garden that have each of them the dew of Heaven, which, being shaken with the wind, they let fall at each other's roots, whereby they are jointly nourished, and become nourishers of each other.—*John Bunyan.*

PRIDE is to character, like the attic to the house—the highest part, and generally the most empty.—*Gay.*

Life is a web, time is a shuttle, and man is a weaver. The principle of action is a thread in the web of life. Of that web, two things are true, that which enters therein will reappear, and nothing will reappear which was not put therein.
—*J. H. Newman.*

THE VIRTUES, like the Muses, are always seen in groups. A good principle was never found solitary in any breast.
—*Jane Porter.*

WORLDLY RICHES are like nuts: many clothes are torn in getting them, many a tooth broken in cracking them, but never a belly filled with eating them.
—*Venning.*

AS THE IVY twines around the oak, so *misery* and *misfortune* encompass the happiness of man. Felicity, pure and unalloyed, is not a plant of earthly growth; her gardens are in the skies.—*Burton.*

A WORLD without a *Sabbath* would be like a man without a smile, like a summer without flowers, and like a homestead without a garden. It is the joyous day of the whole week.—*Beecher.*

THE MAN without *purpose* is like a ship without a rudder—a waif, a nothing, a no man. Have a purpose in life, and, having it, throw such strength of mind and muscle into your work as God has given you.—*Carlyle.*

TEMPTATIONS are a file which rub off much of the rust of our self-confidence.
—*Fenelon.*

ARCHITECTS—Many men build as cathedrals were built—the part nearest the ground finished, but that part which soars toward heaven, the turrets and the spires, forever incomplete. A kitchen, a cellar, a bar and a bedroom, these are the whole of some men, the only apartments in their soul-house. Many men are mere warehouses full of merchandise, the head, the heart stuffed with goods. Like those houses in the lower streets of the city which were once family dwellings, but are now used for commercial purposes, there are apartments in their souls which were once tenanted by taste and love and joy and worship; but they are all deserted now, and the rooms are filled with earthly and material things.
—*Beecher.*

TEARS are often the telescope through which men see far into heaven.
—*Beecher.*

CONSCIENCE—When it has lost its delicate sensibility, and its power of direction, there seems to be only one method of restoration, and that is by placing it alongside of a pure standard of right and wrong, as the magnetized iron which has lost its virtue is restored by being bound up for a time with a correctly pointing magnet.—*McCosh.*

A MAN who hoards up *riches* and enjoys them not is like an ass that carries gold and eats thistles.—*Burton.*

⚏

SORROW is only one of the lower notes in the oratorio of our blessedness.
—*Armistead Gordon.*

⚏

HOPE may be described as the flower of desire. It expects that the object shall be attained. It bars despondence and anticipates good. It shakes the mind from stagnations, and animates to encounter danger, and is the balm of life. Though at times it may be associated with doubt and solicitude, yet when hesitance is displaced, it swells into joy and ecstacy. Hope may be held to be universal and permanent. It is entwined with every other affection and passion. It always originates beneficial effects. It animates desire, and is a secret source of pleasure in the transports of joy. Joy triumphs in the success which hope presages will be permanent. It administers consolation in distress—quickens all our pursuits, and communicates to the mind the pleasure of anticipation. This influence, though mild, is nevertheless exhilarating and salutary. There is no happiness which hope cannot promise, no difficulty which it cannot surmount, no grief which it cannot mitigate. It is the wealth of the indigent, the health of the sick, the freedom of the captive, the rest of the toiler.—*Cuyler.*

⚏

OUR PRAYER and God's mercy are like two buckets in a well; while one ascends, the other descends.—*Hopkins.*

⚏

IT IS with a *word* as with an arrow—once let it loose and it does not return.
—*Abd-el-Kader.*

VIRTUE is like an angel; but she is a blind one and must ask knowledge to show her the pathway that leads to her goal. Mere knowledge, on the other hand, like a Swiss mercenary, is ready to combat either in the ranks of sin or under the banners of righteousness.—*Horace Mann.*

⚏

TRIALS are medicines which our gracious and wise physician prescribes, because we need them; and he proportions the frequency and weight of them to what the case requires. Let us trust his skill and thank him for his prescription.
—*Newton.*

⚏

WORDS are like leaves; and where they most abound, much fruit of sense beneath is seldom found.—*Pope.*

⚏

REASON is like the sun, of which the light is constant, uniform, and lasting; fancy, a meteor of bright but transitory lustre; irregular in its motion and delusive in its direction.—*Johnson.*

⚏

FRAGMENTS

What is poetry? Is it a mosaic
   Of colored stones which curiously are
      wrought
   Into a pattern? Rather glass that's
      taught
By patient labor any hue to take
And glowing with a sumptuous splendor,
      make
   Beauty a thing of awe where sun-
      beams caught,
   Transmitted fall in sheafs of rainbows
      fraught
With storied meaning for religion's sake.
—*Amy Lowell.*

V. APPRECIATION

SPIRITUAL DISCERNMENT — When a man stood before one of Turner's unrivalled paintings and said, "I can see nothing in it," the great artist replied, "Don't you wish you could?" A tourist upon his return home was asked what he thought of Notre Dame, and the Sistine Madonna, and some other of the world's remarkable productions. He said he did not see them, and went on to say that while his wife did the Cathedrals and his daughter did the art galleries, he did the cafes. There are some things that must be spiritually discerned and appreciated, and if eyes are blind, and heart is dull, and the soul desensitized, no wonder it is difficult to appreciate the higher things of God.—*Swift.*

RECOMPENSE — Do right, and God's recompense to you will be the power of doing more right. Give, and God's reward to you will be the spirit of giving more; a blessed spirit, for it is the Spirit of God Himself, whose Life is the blessedness of giving. Love, and God will pay you with the capacity of more love; for love is Heaven—love is God within you.—*F. W. Robertson.*

LOVE AND UNDERSTANDING —I am happy in having learned to distinguish between ownership and possession. Books, pictures, and all the beauty of the world belong to those who love and understand them—not usually to those who possess them. All of these things that I am entitled to I have—I own them by divine right. So I care not a bit who possesses them. I used to care very much and consequently was very unhappy.
—*James Howard Kehler.*

PRAISE—A noted editor once noticed a particularly fine achievement by a friend, also an editor. He thought he would write immediately a letter of congratulation to his friend. But he didn't. There was a day or two of delay, and then he said to himself, "Oh, pshaw! he will get hundreds of other notes about it, so I shall not bother him with mine." Then he met his friend and told him how it happened he had failed to send his letter of commendation. "How many do you think I did receive?" asked the friend. The editor guessed many scores. But the real answer was, "Not one."
—*John T. Faris.*

IF I HAD THE TIME

If I had the time to find a place
And sit me down full face to face
  With my better self, that stands no
    show
  In my daily life that rushes so,
It might be then I would see my soul
Was stumbling still toward the shin-
    ing goal—
  I might be nerved by the thought
    sublime,
    If I had the time!

If I had the time to learn from you
How much for comfort my word would
    do;
  And I told you then of my sudden
    will
  To kiss your feet when I did you ill—
If the tears aback of the bravado
Could force their way and let you
    know—
  Brothers, the souls of us all would
    chime,
    If we had the time!

—RICHARD BURTON.

31

ASK Him to increase your powers of sympathy: to give you more quickness and depth of sympathy, in little things as well as great. Opportunities of doing a kindness are often lost from mere want of thought. Half a dozen lines of kindness may bring sunshine into the whole day of some sick person. Think of the pleasure you might give to some one who is much shut up, and who has fewer pleasures than you have, by sharing with her some little comfort or enjoyment that you have learned to look upon as a necessary of life,—the pleasant drive, the new book, flowers from the country, etc. Try to put yourself in another's place. Ask "What should I like myself, if I were hard-worked, or sick, or lonely?" Cultivate the habit of sympathy.

—*G. H. Wilkinson.*

UNKINDNESS—Go to the grave of buried love, and meditate. There settle thy account with thy conscience for every past benefit unrequited, every past endearment unregarded, of that departed being, who can never, never return to be soothed by thy contrition. If thou art a husband, and hast ever caused that fond bosom that ventured its whole happiness in thy arms to doubt one moment of thy kindness or thy truth; if thou hast ever wronged in thought, in word, or deed, the spirit that generously confided in thee; if thou hast ever given one unremitted pang to that true heart which now lies cold and still beneath thy feet, then be sure that every unkind look, every ungracious word, every ungentle action will come thronging back upon thy memory, and knocking dolefully at thy soul. Then be sure that thou wilt lie down sorrowing and repentant at the grave, and utter the unheard groan, and pour the unavailing tear, more deep, more bitter because

unavailing. Then weave thy chaplet of flowers, and strew the beauties of nature about the grave; console thy broken spirit, if thou canst, with those tender but futile tributes of regret; but take warning by the bitterness of this thy contrite affliction over the dead, and be more faithful and affectionate in the duties to the living.

—*Irving.*

GIVE THEM THE FLOWERS NOW

Closed eyes can't see the white roses,
  Cold hands can't hold them, you know,
Breath that is stilled can not gather
  The odors that sweet from them blow
Death, with a peace beyond dreaming,
  Its children of earth doth endow;
Life is the time we can help them,
  So give them the flowers now!

Here are the struggles and striving,
  Here are the cares and the tears;
Now is the time to be smoothing
  The frowns and the furrows and fear,
What to closed eyes are kind sayings?
  What to hushed heart is deep vow?
Naught can avail after parting,
  So give them the flowers now!

Just a kind word or a greeting;
  Just a warm grasp or a smile—
There are the flowers that will lighten
  The burdens for many a mile.
After the journey is over
  What is the use of them; how
Can they carry them who must be carried?
  Oh, give them the flowers now!

Blooms from the happy heart's garden
  Plucked in the spirit of love;
Blooms that are earthly reflections
  Of flowers that blossom above.
Words cannot tell what a measure
  Of blessing such gifts will allow
To dwell in the lives of many,
  So give them the flowers now!

—*Leigh M. Hodges.*

DEBTORS—When Paul said, "I am a debtor to both the Greeks and to the barbarians, both to the wise and to the unwise," he did not mean that he had received anything from them for which he was bound to pay them. He had never bought anything in their markets without giving its price; neither had they lent him any sums on interest. No human being had any pecuniary claim against him. Neither did he owe to Greek or barbarian any gratitude for favors which he had received at their hands, for in almost every city in which he labored he had encountered persecution and suffered wrong.

Not, therefore, on the ground of anything which he had obtained from them, but solely on the ground of that which he had received from another for them, does he acknowledge himself the debtor. "The glorious Gospel of the blessed God" had been "committed" to his "trust;" he had been "allowed of God to be put in trust with the Gospel" for their benefit, and therefore, that he might be a faithful steward of the mysteries of God, he was exceedingly desirous of preaching the truth, as it is in Jesus, to men of every nation and of every degree. He could not honestly hold it back. It had not been given to him for himself alone; and if he had attempted to keep it from his fellow-men, he would have been guilty of the greatest defalcation, and could not have vindicated himself either at the bar of conscience, or at the bar of God.

This explains the earnestness, the perseverance, and the self-sacrifice of his missionary life.—*Cuyler.*

INDIFFERENCE—It is a sad thing to reflect that in a world so overflowing with goodness of smell, of fine sights and sweet sounds, we pass by hastily and take so little note of them.—*David Grayson.*

KIND—The Christian surely means to be considerate and kind in Heaven! But why not here on earth and in these trying circumstances where perhaps his friends and neighbors need it most?
—*Bolton Jones.*

WORKING WITH GOD—If I can put one touch of rosy sunset into the life of any man or woman, I shall feel that I have worked with God.
—*George Macdonald.*

ONE IN TEN—There were ten lepers healed, and only one turned back to give thanks, but it is to be noticed that our Lord did not recall His gift from the other nine because of their lack of gratitude. When we begin to lessen our acts of kindness and helpfulness because we think those who receive do not properly appreciate what is done for them, it is time to question our own motives.

TOO LATE—There is a wealth of unexpressed love in the world. It is one of the chief causes of sorrow evoked by death: what might have been said or might have been done that never can be said or done.—*Arthur Hopkins.*

A Rose to the Living

A rose to the living is more
   Than sumptuous wreaths to the dead;
In filling love's infinite store,
   A rose to the living is more
If graciously given before
   The hungering spirit is fled—
A rose to the living is more,
   Than sumptuous wreaths to the dead.
—*Nixon Waterman.*

THE ALABASTER BOX—Do not keep the alabaster box of your love and friendship sealed up until your friends are dead. Fill their lives with sweetness. Speak approving, cheering words while their ears can hear them, and while their hearts can be thrilled and made happier. The kind things you mean to say when they are gone, say before they go.

—*George W. Childs.*

THANKFULNESS—First among the things to be thankful for is a thankful spirit. Some people would grumble at the accommodations in Heaven if they ever got there. They take their blessings here so much as a matter of course, that even a day of general thanksgiving once in a year is more than they feel any need of. And if their personal blessings in any measure fail, gratitude for what they have had or still enjoy is the last thing they think of. Another class really desire to be thankful, but they are naturally despondent. Their sky is as dark with clouds as though a special Old Probabilities were employed to keep it full. They go through the world in a deprecating spirit, hoping things may turn out well yet fearing for the worst. We always feel glad for this class when Thanksgiving Day comes around. They then have an official warrant for gratitude. If their own hearts do not formulate blessings, they can listen to the sermon, or look to the President's proclamation.

How different with the thankful heart! What a gift it is to be born with an outlook toward the bright side of things! And if not so by nature, what a triumph of grace to be made thankful through a renewed heart! It is so much more comfortable and rational to see what we have to be thankful for and to rejoice accordingly, than to have our vision for ever filled with our lacks and our needs. Happy are they who possess this gift! Blessings may fail and fortunes vary, but the thankful heart remains. The happy past, at least, is secure—and Heaven is ahead.

—*Golden Rule.*

GRATITUDE

O Thou, whose bounty fills my cup
  With every blessing meet!
I give Thee thanks for every drop—
  The bitter and the sweet.
I praise Thee for the desert road,
  And for the riverside;
For all Thy goodness hath bestowed,
  And all Thy grace denied.

—*Jane Crewdson.*

WASTED OPPORTUNITY—Ruskin once said that when we fail to praise a man who deserves praise, two sad things happen; we run a chance of driving him from the right road for want of encouragement, and we deprive ourselves of one of the very happiest of our privileges, the privilege of rewarding labor that deserves a reward.

High thoughts and noble in all lands
  Help me; my soul is fed by such.
But ah, the touch of lips and hands—
  The human touch!
Warm, vital, close, life's symbols dear,—
These need I most, and now, and here.

—*Richard Burton.*

"Shut in with God! O wondrous thought:
Shut in with the peace his sufferings
    brought;
Shut in with the love that wields the rod:
O company blest! Shut in with God!"

VI. ASPIRATION

BUILDING TEMPLES — The Bible tells of dreamers, and among the most conspicuous was Joseph. He told his dreams to his brothers, and his brothers hated him because of his dreams. One day when his father sent him out where his brothers were keeping their flocks in Dothan, they saw him coming afar off and said: "Behold, the dreamer cometh." They plotted to kill him—and he is not the only dreamer who has been plotted against in this old world. But finally they decided that instead of killing him they would put him down in a pit; but some merchants passing that way, the brothers decided to sell him to the merchants, and the merchants carried Joseph down into Egypt.

Time went on and the brothers had almost forgotten the dreamer Joseph. But a famine came,—yes a famine,—and then they had to go down into Egypt, and buy corn, and when they got there, they found the dreamer—and he had the corn. So I decided that it was not so bad after all for one to be a dreamer—if one has the corn.

But the more I thought of the dreamer's place in history, the less I felt entitled to the distinction. John Boyle O'Reilly says that: "The dreamer lives forever, while the toiler dies in a day."

In traveling through Europe you find great cathedrals. An architect had a vision of a temple of worship and he put that vision upon paper. Then the builders began, and they laid stone upon stone and brick upon brick, until finally the temple was completed—completed sometimes centuries after the dreamer's death. And people now travel from all corners of the world to look upon the temple, and the name of the dreamer is known while the names of the toilers are forgotten.

No, I cannot claim a place among the dreamers, but there has been a great dreamer in the realm of statesmanship— Thomas Jefferson. He saw a people bowed beneath oppression and he had a vision of a self-governing nation, in which every citizen would be a sovereign. He put his vision upon paper, and for more than a century multitudes have been building. They are building at this temple in every nation; some day it will be completed and then the people of all the world will find protection beneath its roof and security within its walls. I shall be content if, when my days are numbered, it can be truthfully said of me that with such ability as I possessed, and whenever opportunity offered, I labored faithfully with the multitude to build this building higher in my time.

—*William Jennings Bryan.*

GOD THE ARCHITECT

Who Thou art I know not
  But this much I know;
Thou hast set the Pleiades
  In a silver row;

Thou hast sent the trackless winds
  Loose upon their way;
Thou hast reared a colored wall
  Twixt the night and day;

Thou hast made the flowers to bloom
  And the stars to shine;
Hid rare gems of richest ore
  In the tunneled mine;

But chief of all Thy wondrous works,
  Supreme of all Thy plan,
Thou hast put an upward reach
  Into the heart of man.

—HARRY KEMP.

VISION—It was sagacious Thomas Carlyle who said that the man who cannot wonder, who does not habitually wonder and worship, though he were president of innumerable royal societies, and carried the whole *Mechanique Celeste* and Hegel's philosophy and the epitome of all laboratories and observatories, with their results, in his single head, is but *a pair of spectacles behind which there is no eye.*

PRAYER

God, though this life is but a wraith,
Although we know not what we use;
Although we grope with little faith,
Give me the heart to fight—and lose.

Ever insurgent let me be,
Make me more daring than devout;
From sleek contentment keep me free,
And fill me with a buoyant doubt.

Open my eyes to visions girt
With beauty, and with wonder lit—
But let me always see the dirt,
And all that spawn and die in it.

Open my ears to music, let
Me thrill with Spring's first flutes and
drums—

But never let me dare forget
The bitter ballads of the slums.

From compromise and things half-done,
Keep me, with stern and stubborn pride;
And when, at last, the fight is won,
God, keep me still unsatisfied.
                              —*Louis Untermeyer.*

From CHALLENGE by Louis Untermeyer, copyright, 1914, by Harcourt, Brace and Company, Inc. Reprinted by permission.

FAILURE—The men who try to do something and fail are infinitely better than those who try to do nothing and succeed.—*Lloyd Jones.*

THE DREAMERS—They are the architects of greatness. Their vision lies within their souls. They never see the mirages of Fact, but peer beyond the veils and mists of doubt and pierce the walls of unborn Time.

Makers of empire, they have fought for bigger things than crowns and higher seats than thrones.

They are the Argonauts, the seekers of the priceless fleece—the Truth.

Through all the ages they have heard the voice of destiny call to them from the unknown vasts.

Their brains have wrought all human miracles. In lace of stone their spires stab the Old World's skies and with their golden crosses kiss the sun.

They are a chosen few—the blazers of the way—who never wear doubt's bandage on their eyes—who starve and chill and hurt, but hold to courage and to hope, because they know that there is always proof of truth for them who try— that only cowardice and lack of faith can keep the seeker from his chosen goal, but if his heart be strong and if he dream enough and dream it hard enough, he can attain, no matter where men failed before.

Walls crumble and the empires fall. The tidal wave sweeps from the sea and tears a fortress from its rocks. The rotting nations drop from off Time's bough, and only things the dreamers make live on.

They are the Eternal Conquerors— their vassals are the years.
                              —*Herbert Kaufman.*

STAR GAZERS—Ideals are like stars, you will not succeed in touching them with your hands, but like the seafaring man on the desert of waters, you choose them as your guides, and, following them, you reach your destiny—*Carl Schurz.*

CONSIDER FUNDAMENTALS.— Utopia has long been another name for the unreal and the impossible. . . . As a matter of fact, it is our Utopias that make the world tolerable to us: the cities and mansions that people dream of are those in which they finally live . . . What makes human history such an uncertain and fascinating story is that man lives in two worlds—the world within and the world without . . . In the midst of the tepid and half-hearted discussions that continue to arise . . . let us break in with the injunction to talk about fundamentals—consider Utopia!

—*Lewis Mumford.*

UPWARD — Nothwithstanding the sight of all our miseries, which press upon us and take us by the throat, we have an instinct which we cannot repress, and which lifts us up.—*Pascal.*

HERE OR NOWHERE—Here in this poor, miserable, hampered, despicable Actual, wherein thou now standest, here or nowhere is thy Ideal; work it out therefrom, and working, believe, live, be free.— O thou that pinest in the imprisonment of the Actual, and criest bitterly to the gods for a kingdom wherein to rule and create, know this for a truth: the thing thou seekest is already here, "here or nowhere," couldst thou only see.—*Thomas Carlyle.*

THE IDEAL LIFE is in our blood and never will be still. Sad will be the day for any man when he becomes contented with the thoughts he is thinking and the deeds he is doing,—where there is not forever beating at the doors of his soul some great desire to do something larger, which he knows that he was meant and made to do.—*Phillips Brooks.*

AIM HIGH — Success lies, not in achieving what you aim at, but in aiming at what you ought to achieve, and pressing forward, sure of achievement here, or if not here, hereafter.—*R. F. Horton.*

HILLS

I never loved your plains!—
　　Your gentle valleys,
Your drowsy country lanes
　　And pleached alleys.

I want my hills!—the trail
　　That scorns the hollow.
Up, up the ragged shale
　　Where few will follow,

Up, over wooded crest
　　And mossy bowlder
With strong thigh, heaving chest,
　　And swinging shoulder,

So let me hold my way,
　　By nothing halted,
Until, at close of day,
　　I stand, exalted,

High on my hills of dream—
　　Dear hills that know me!
And then, how fair will seem
　　The lands below me.

How pure, at vesper-time,
　　The far bells chiming!
God, give me hills to climb,
　　And strength for climbing!
　　　　　　—*Arthur Guiterman.*

Taken from DEATH AND GENERAL PUTNAM, by Arthur Guiterman, published and copyright by E. P. Dutton & Co., Inc., New York, 1935.

PURSUIT OF THE IDEAL — Our duty to God is to make of ourselves the most perfect product of divine incarnation that we can become. This is possible only through the pursuit of worthy ideals.

—*Edgar White Burrill.*

DARE GREATLY—It is not the critic who counts; not the man who points out how the strong man stumbled, or where the doer of deeds could have done better. The credit belongs to the man who is actually in the arena; whose face is marred by dust and sweat and blood; who strives valiantly; who errs and comes short again and again; who knows the great enthusiasms, the great devotions, and spends himself in a worthy cause; who at the best knows in the end the triumph of high achievement; and who at the worst, if he fails, at least fails while daring greatly; so that his place shall never be with those cold and timid souls who know neither victory nor defeat.—*Theodore Roosevelt.*

Victory

Attempt the end, and never stand to doubt,
Nothing's so hard but search will find it out.

—*Herrick.*

EMERSON SAID: "Hitch your wagon to a star." One can see in those six little words the summary of human achievement, and an everlasting inspiration to the future races of men. From Socrates to Edison, every forward step taken by mankind through revolving centuries, every advance by humanity towards the ultimate goal, has been led by some valiant dreamer whose eyes were fixed upon the dawn. Moses, with dying eyes, saw a star that blazed in the Promised Land; the radiance of an eternal star led Three Wise Men to the manger in Bethlehem; Columbus pinned his faith in the dawn of a new day; Kepler, announcing the laws of the unchanging spheres; Newton, watching the apple fall, each looked beyond, and into the future.

—*J. E. Dinger.*

WHAT MEN LIVE BY—Not long before his death Renan said that one could not do a finer service to mankind than to preach constantly that man doth not live by bread alone. We cannot too soon learn that the saving power in civilization is not coal or wheat or wool, but elements more ideal.—*Clarke.*

CREEDS—We find in our study of social development three human creeds: First, might makes right; second, knowledge is power; third, goodness is greatness. Humanity has outgrown its first creed, is distrusting the second, and is apprehending the third. Under the first, monarchy was the form of government. Under the second, aristocracy. Under the third, democracy will appear. Under the first the warrior was king, under the second the philosopher. Under the third, the servant will be master. In the light of eternity past I read that a man's greatness was measured by his ability to make the world serve him, but in the light of eternity to come a man's greatness will be measured by his ability to serve his fellowmen. Under the monarchy there were slaves. Under the aristocracy, there were wage earners. Under the democracy all will be fellow-workers. You may call this a Utopian dream, but it is the logic of events. It is the program of the inevitable. It is the march of the centuries. Caesar and Plato must pass on, and Christ will be supreme.

—*Christian Evangelist.*

DREAMS do come true, if we only wish hard enough. You can have anything in life if you will sacrifice everything else for it. "What will you have?" says God. "Pay for it and take it."

—*James Barrie.*

IDEALS — Now, believe me, God hides some ideal in every human soul. At some time in our life we feel a trembling, fearful longing to do some good thing. Life finds its noblest spring of excellence in this hidden impulse to do our best. There is a time when we are not content to be such merchants or doctors or lawyers as we see on the dead level or below it. The woman longs to glorify her womanhood as sister, wife, or mother. Here is God,—God standing silently at the door all day long.—*Robert Collyer.*

THE WAY TO UTOPIA—Before men can come to Utopia, they must learn the way there. Utopia, I see, is only a home for those who have learnt the way . . . it is not the place for men who grow wealthy by intercepting but by serving.
—*H. G. Wells.*

UPWARD

Glad that I live am I;
  That the sky is blue;
Glad for the country lanes,
  And the fall of dew.

After the sun, the rain.
  After the rain, the sun,
This is the way of life
  Till the work is done.

All that we need to do,
  Be we low or high
Is to see that we grow
  Nearer the sky.

From THE SELECTED POEMS OF LIZETTE WOODWORTH REESE, copyright, 1926, by Lizette Woodworth Reese, and reprinted by permission of Rinehart & Company, Inc., Publishers.

SOWERS—A handful of pine-seed will cover mountains with the green majesty of forests. I too will set my face to the wind and throw my handful of seed on high.—*Fiona Macleod.*

THE TRUER LIFE

No star is ever lost we once have seen,
We always may be what we might have
  been.
Since Good, though only thought, has
  life and breath,
God's life—can always be redeemed from
  death;
And evil, in its nature, is decay,
And any hour can blot it all away;
The hopes that lost in some far distance
  seen,
May be the truer life, and this the dream.
      —*Adelaide Ann Procter.*

FOUNDATIONS—If you have built castles in the air, your work need not be lost; that is where they should be. Now put the foundations under them.
      —*Thoreau.*

CASTLES IN THE AIR—I find the gayest castles in the air that were ever piled far better for comfort and for use than the dungeons in the air that are daily dug and caverned out by grumbling, discontented people. A man should make life and nature happier to us, or he had better never been born.—*Emerson.*

He . . . loved to weave
Dream warp and woof more fair than
    things that are.
He made believe . . . that far beyond the
    goal
That lures our eyes, to nobler ports we
    steer;
That grief was meant to forge the living
    soul,
And death itself is not for men to fear . . .
So well he made believe, he really made
The world believe his make-believes
    were true.

Taken from DEATH AND GENERAL PUTNAM, by Arthur Guiterman, published and copyright by E. P. Dutton & Co., Inc., New York, 1935.

VII. BEAUTY

THE FOUNTAIN—All beauty is a gleam from the fountain of beauty. No work of beauty can be more beautiful than the mind which designed it. I do not think a sculptor can possibly chisel a marble so as to make it more beautiful than his own ideal conception. I do not think a painter can produce a painting more beautiful than the thought of his mind which led up to it; I do not think a musician can express in sound, or a poet on paper, anything beyond the thought within him. I know, indeed, that the conception of either may grow with the process by which it is presented to others, and that the man may, as he proceeds, have a fairer and nobler view of what he is trying to express; but, after all, the mind of the sculptor is more beautiful than the marble which he has sculptured; and the mind of the painter is a more beautiful thing than the work of art which he has painted; and the mind of the musician is better and higher and nobler than the most exquisite symphony which he has composed and reduced to writing; and the mind of the poet is better than his most beautiful piece of poetry. And so we must rise from all the fragments of beauty which God has scattered so widely over His world to say with Milton—

"Thine this universal frame
Thus wondrous fair; Thyself how wondrous then!"

—*E. H. Bickersteth.*

EXPRESSION—Beauty does not lie in the face. It lies in the harmony between man and his industry. Beauty is expression. When I paint a mother I try to render her beautiful by the mere look she gives her child.—*Jean Francois Millet.*

THE MIRROR OF THE SOUL—Goodness and love mould the form into their own image, and cause the joy and beauty of love to shine forth from every part of the face. When this form of love is seen, it appears ineffably beautiful, and affects with delight the inmost life of the soul.—*E. Swedenborg.*

COMPLEXION HINT—There is no beautifier of complexion, or form, or behavior, like the wish to scatter joy and not pain around us.—*Ralph Waldo Emerson.*

GOOD LOOKS—Cheerfulness and content are great beautifiers and are famous preservers of youthful looks.

—*Charles Dickens.*

BARTER

Life has loveliness to sell,
  All beautiful and splendid things,
Blue waves whitened on a cliff,
  Soaring fire that sways and sings,
And children's faces looking up
Holding wonder like a cup.

Life has loveliness to sell,
  Music like a curve of gold,
Scent of pine trees in the rain,
  Eyes that love you, arms that hold,
And for your spirit's still delight,
Holy thoughts that star the night.

Spend all you have for loveliness,
  Buy it and never count the cost;
For one white singing hour of peace
  Count many a year of strife well lost,
And for a breath of ectasy
Give all you have been, or could be.

—SARA TEASDALE.

From THE COLLECTED POEMS of Sara Teasdale. By permission of The Macmillan Company, publishers.

Bible

The Bible is a window
in this prison of hope,
through which we look
into eternity. —*Dwight.*

DAYSTAR AND DAWN—Our fair morning is at hand; the daystar is near the rising, and we are not many miles from home. What matter, then, of ill-entertainment in the smoky inns of this worthless world? We are not to stay here, and we shall be dearly welcome to Him to whom we are going.—*Samuel Rutherford.*

THE TEMPLE OF BEAUTY—Beauty is an all-pervading presence. It unfolds to the numberless flowers of the Spring; it waves in the branches of the trees and in the green blades of grass; it haunts the depths of the earth and the sea, and gleams out in the hues of the shell and the precious stone. And not only these minute objects, but the ocean, the mountains, the clouds, the heavens, the stars, the rising and the setting sun, all overflow with beauty. The universe is its temple; and those men who are alive to it can not lift their eyes without feeling themselves encompassed with it on every side. Now, this beauty is so precious, the enjoyment it gives so refined and pure, so congenial and so akin to worship, that it is pain living in the midst of it, and living almost as blind to it, as if, instead of this fair earth and glorious sky, they were tenants of a dungeon. An infinite joy is lost to the world by the want of culture of this spiritual endowment. The greatest truths are wronged if not linked with beauty, and they win their way most surely and deeply into the soul when arrayed in this their natural and fit attire.
—*W. E. Channing.*

TRIALS

I would not miss one single tear,
  Heart pang, or throbbing brow;
Sweet was the chastisement severe,
  And sweet its memory now.
—*Amelia E. Barr.*

THE GREATER THING

Great it is to believe the dream
When we stand in youth by the starry
  stream;
But a greater thing is to fight life through
And say at the end, "The dream was
  true."
—*Edwin Markham.*
Reprinted by permission.

GOODNESS—Did it ever strike you that goodness is not merely a beautiful thing, but by far the most beautiful thing in the whole world? So that nothing is to be compared for value with goodness; that riches, honor, power, pleasure, learning, the whole world and all in it, are not worth having in comparison with being good; and the utterly best thing for a man is to be good, even though he were never to be rewarded for it.—*Charles Kingsley.*

ETERNITY AFFIRMS THE HOUR

All we have willed or hoped or dreamed
  of good shall exist;
  Not its semblance, but itself; no beauty,
  nor good, nor power
Whose voice has gone forth, but each
  survives for the melodist
  When eternity affirms the conception
  of an hour.
The high that proved too high, the heroic
  for earth too hard,
  The passion that left the ground to love
  itself in the sky,
Are music sent up to God by the lover
  and the bard;
  Enough that he heard it once: we shall
  hear it by and by.
—*Robert Browning.*

FAR AWAY there in the sunshine are my highest aspirations. I may not reach them, but I can look up and see their beauty, believe in them, and try to follow where they lead.—*Louisa May Alcott.*

TO CULTIVATE the sense of the beautiful, is one of the most effectual ways of cultivating an appreciation of the divine goodness.—*Bovee.*

BEAUTY OF FORM affects the mind, but then it must not be the mere shell that we admire, but the thought that this shell is only the beautiful case adjusted to the shape and value of a still more beautiful pearl within.—The perfection of outward loveliness is the soul shining through its crystalline covering.
—*Jane Porter.*

WALKING WITH GOD—There is only one basis for really enjoying life, and that is, to walk in the way in which God leads you. Then you are prepared to find delight in all sorts of wayside incidents.

For one thing, the ability of the senses to enjoy anything depends as much on the tone of the mind as on any external happening. Some people are like Peter Bell of whom Wordsworth wrote:

"A primrose by a river's brim
A yellow primrose was to him,
And it was nothing more."

When a man is drifting through life, seeking nothing outside of self-gratification, the world must become increasingly a barren and forbidding wilderness.

But it is wonderful how many delights fall to the lot of him who is led by God. For such a one the clasp of a friends' hand, a cool drink in the heat of noon, a merry salutation from a passing traveler, a glimpse of beauty by the road, a quiet resting-place at night, are all full of unspeakable pleasure.

JUST A BIT—If the nose of Cleopatra had been a little shorter, it would have changed the history of the world.—*Pascal.*

ACID TEST—The criterion of true beauty is, that it increases on examination; if false, that it lessens.—There is therefore, something in true beauty that corresponds with right reason, and is not the mere creation of fancy.—*Greville.*

BEAUTY is as summer fruits, which are easy to corrupt and cannot last; and for the most part it makes a dissolute youth, and an age a little out of countenance; but if it light well, it makes virtues shine and vice blush.—*Bacon.*

CHEAP LUXURY—No man receives the full culture of a man in whom the sensibility to the beautiful is not cherished; and there is no condition of life from which it should be excluded.—Of all luxuries this the cheapest, and the most at hand, and most important to those conditions where coarse labor tends to give grossness to the mind.—*Channing.*

EVERY YEAR of my life I grow more convinced that it is wisest and best to fix our attention on the beautiful and the good, and dwell as little as possible on the evil and the false.—*Cecil.*

MENTAL PICTURES—One of the most practical things a man can do with his holidays and leisure time is to store his mind with pictures of beauty and truth. By discriminating thought, conversation, observation, he may lay up hidden sources of strength and grace.

CRITERION—That which is striking and beautiful is not always good; but that which is good is always beautiful.
—*Ninon de l'Enclos.*

MANY CHARMS—Beauty hath so many charms one knows not how to speak against it; and when a graceful figure is the habitation of a virtuous soul—when the beauty of the face speaks out the modesty and humility of the mind, it raises our thoughts up to the great Creator; but after all, beauty, like truth, is never so glorious as when it goes the plainest.
—Sterne.

BEAUTY AND TRUTH—The most natural beauty in the world is honesty and moral truth.—For all beauty is truth.— True features make the beauty of the face; true proportions, the beauty of architecture; true measures, the beauty of harmony and music.—Shaftesbury.

REMEDY—There is no more potent antidote to low sensuality than the adoration of beauty.—All the higher arts of design are essentially chaste.—They purify the thoughts, as tragedy, according to Aristotle, purifies the passions.—Schlegel.

EVERY TRAIT of beauty may be referred to some virtue, as to innocence, candor, generosity, modesty, or heroism.
—St. Pierre.

AFTER ALL, it is the divinity within that makes the divinity without; and I have been more fascinated by a woman of talent and intelligence, though deficient in personal charms, than I have been by the most regular beauty.
—Washington Irving.

BEAUTY is but the sensible image of the Infinite.—Like truth and justice it lives within us; like virtue and the moral law it is a companion of the soul.—Bancroft.

THE MIDDLE WAY — The finest lives, in my opinion, are those who rank in the common model, and with the human race, but without miracle, without extravagance.—Montaigne.

THE BEAUTY SEEN is partly in him who sees it.—Bovee.

COURSES—To give pain is the tyranny; to make happy, the true empire of beauty.—Steele.

HINDSIGHT—What we have, we prize, not to the worth while we enjoy it; but being lacked and lost, why then we reck the value; then we find the virtue that possession would not show us while it was ours.—Shakespeare.

DEFINING—Socrates called beauty a short-lived tyranny; Plato, a privilege of nature; Theophrastus, a silent cheat; Theocritus, a delightful prejudice; Carneades, a solitary kingdom; Aristotle, that it was better than all the letters of recommendation in the world; Homer, that it was a glorious gift of nature, and Ovid, that it was a favor bestowed by the gods.

The fountain of beauty is the heart, and every generous thought illustrates the walls of your chamber.

If virtue accompanies beauty it is the heart's paradise; if vice be associate with it, it is the soul's purgatory.—It is the wise man's bonfire, and the fool's furnace.
—Quarles.

EVEN VIRTUE is more fair when it appears in a beautiful person.—Virgil.

THE BEST PART of beauty is that which no picture can express.—Bacon.

VIII. THE BIBLE

ENLIGHTENMENT.—The Bible as a book stands alone. There never was, nor ever will be, another like it. As there is but one sun to enlighten the world naturally, so there is but one Book to enlighten the world spiritually. May that Book become to each of us the man of our counsel, the guide of our journey, the inspiration of our thought, and our support and comfort in life and in death.

—A. Galloway.

The Bible contains 3,566,480 letters, 733,746 words, 31,163 verses, 1,189 chapters and 66 books. The longest chapter is the 119th Psalm; shortest, the middle chapter, the 117th Psalm. The middle verse is the 8th of the 118th Psalm. The longest name is in the 8th chapter of Isaiah. The word "and" occurs 46,227 times; the word Jehovah 6,855 times. The thirty-seventh chapter of Isaiah and the 19th chapter of the 2nd book of Kings are alike. The longest verse is the 9th of the 8th chapter of Esther; the shortest verse is the 35th of the 11th chapter of John. In the 21st verse of the 7th chapter of Ezra is the alphabet. The finest piece of reading is the 26th chapter of Acts. The name of God is not mentioned in the book of Esther. The Bible contains two testaments. The Old is Law, The New is Love. The Old is the Bud, The New is the Bloom. In the Old, man is reaching up for God. In the New, God is reaching down for man. In the Old, man is in the valley but can see the sun shining on the mountain tops. In the New he is on the mountain top basking in the sunlight of God's infinite love.

SHEPHERD.—Who is it that is your shepherd? The Lord! Oh, my friends, what a wonderful announcement! The Lord God of Heaven and Earth, the almighty Creator of all things, He who holds the universe in His hand as though it were a very little thing,—He is your shepherd, and has charged Himself with the care and keeping of you, as a shepherd is charged with the care and keeping of his sheep. If your hearts could really take in this thought, you would never have a fear or a care again; for with such a shepherd, how could it be possible for you ever to want any good thing?

—H. W. Smith.

DIFFICULTIES.— Believe the Bible and thou shalt be saved. No. There is no such word written. It is "Believe on the Lord Jesus Christ and thou shalt be saved." Do not trouble yourself in the first instance about questions connected with the book of Genesis, or difficulties suggested by the book of Revelation. Let the wars of the Jews alone in the meantime, and dismiss Jonah from your mind. Look to Jesus: get acquainted with Him —listen to His word—believe in Him— trust Him—obey Him. This is all that is asked of you in the first instance. After you have believed on Christ, and taken Him as your Savior, your Master, your Model, you will not be slow to find out that "all Scripture is given by inspiration of God, and is profitable for doctrine, and for reproof, and for correction, and for instruction in godliness." You may never have all your difficulties solved, or all your objections met, but you will be sure of your foundation; you will feel that your feet are planted on the "Rock of Ages."

—Gibson.

PREACHERS—Strong preachers have ever been Bible preachers. The old Reformers drew their weapons from the heavenly armory. The sermons of Bunyan, and Baxter, and Flavel, and men of their stamp, were full of God—instinct with living doctrines. Their very garb was after the Scripture pattern. Whitefield, as a custom, read the Bible with Henry's Commentary, day by day, on his knees, praying over every sentence, line, and word. Edward and Davies were mighty in the Scriptures. Of Chalmers, it has been said, that his sermons "held the Bible in solution." Preachers who saturate their sermons with the word of God never wear out. The manna which they bring is pure, and sweet, and freshly gathered. It never cloys. God's word is deep, and he who studies it will ever have something new. He will never be dull, for the words of the Bible are strong, living words, and its images and descriptions are very flowers of elegance. Apt citations clinch the passages of the preacher's discourse, and give sanction, dignity, positiveness, authority to it. And they shed light into his subject, like windows in houses.—*Fish.*

INEXHAUSTIBLE—Some one describes packing his bag for a journey. Just before closing it, he observes a small corner not yet filled. He says, "Into this little corner I put a guide-book, a lamp, a mirror, a microscope, a telescope, a volume of choice poems, several well written biographies, a package of old letters, a book of songs, a sharp sword and a small library of more than sixty volumes; yet, strange enough to say, all these did not occupy a space of more than three inches long by two inches wide." "But how could you do it?" "Well, it was all in the packing, I put in my Bible."—*Selected.*

SCRIPTURES—A bright little boy once took the Bible from the center-table of his father's home and turned its dusty pages and said: "Mother, is this God's Book?" "Certainly," was the good mother's reply. "Well, I think we had better send it back to God, for we don't use it here," said the little fellow. This is a fair picture of many a home and the way the Bible is treated. The center-table Bible is a catch-all. It is a place for relics, letters, poetry and pressed flowers. He has revealed to us words of truth and grace, and like David, we should meditate upon His word by day and by night. The Scriptures are sufficient to make us wise unto salvation. Christ says, we are sanctified by them. Paul says, we are begotten by them. Peter says, we are born again by them.
—*Public Speakers Library.*

HANDBOOK OF CIVILIZATION—The Bible has made an ineffaceable impression upon child life. Upon it poets have fed their genius. Its thoughts lie like threads of gold upon the rich pages of each Macaulay or Burke. Orators have quoted from it so largely that we may say that, in proportion as men are cultured, have they been students of the Bible. Today its moral principles form the very substance and body of modern law and jurisprudence. For centuries it has been the book for patriots and reformers; it has been the slave's book; it has been the book for the common people struggling upward; it has been the book of hope for all prodigals; it has been a medicine book for the heart-broken, while its ideas furnish goals for society's future progress. For the individual it teaches the art of individual worth, and is a guide to conduct and character. For the state it is a handbook of universal civilization.
—*Hillis.*

SHEPHERD—The Shepherd knows what pastures are best for His sheep, and they must not question nor doubt, but trustingly follow Him. Perhaps He sees that the best pastures for some of us are to be found in the midst of opposition or of earthly trials. If He leads you there, you may be sure they are green for you, and you will grow and be made strong by feeding there. Perhaps He sees that the best waters for you to walk beside will be raging waves of trouble and sorrow. If this should be the case, He will make them still waters for you, and you must go and lie down beside them, and let them have all their blessed influences upon you.—*H. W. Smith.*

READ—When in sorrow, read John 14.

When men fail you, Psalm 27.

When you have sinned, Psalm 51.

When you worry, Matthew 6:19-34.

Before church service, Psalm 84.

When you are in danger, Psalm 91.

When you have the blues, Psalm 34.

When God seems far away, Psalm 139.

When you are discouraged, Isaiah 40.

If you desire to be fruitful, John 15.

When doubts come upon you, John 7:17.

When you are lonely or fearful, Psalm 33.

When you forget your blessings, Psalm 103.

For Jesus' idea of a Christian, Matthew 5.

For James' idea of religion, James 1:19-27.

For stirring of faith, Hebrews 11.

When you feel down and out, Romans 8:31-39.

When you lack courage for your task, Joshua 1.

When the world seems bigger than God, Psalm 90.

When you want Christian assurance, Romans 8:1-30.

When you leave home for labor or travel, Psalm 121.

When you grow bitter or critical, I Cor. 13.

For Paul's idea of Christianity, II Cor. 5:15-19.

For Paul's rules on how to get along with men, Romans 12.

—Selected.

BE STILL—"Be still, and know that I am God."—Ps. 46:10.

It is not easy to be still in this rough and restless world. Yet God says, "Be still;" and He says also, "In returning and rest shall ye be saved; in quietness and confidence shall be your strength" (Isa. 30:15).

1. Be still, and thou shalt know I can put all enemies to shame. "He that sitteth in the Heavens shall laugh; the Lord shall hold them in derision. Who shall contend with Him who made the Heavens and the earth?" He is still God.

2. Be still, and thou shalt know that I can uphold My own truth in a day of error. Is not My truth precious to Me? and My Book of truth, is it not above all books in Mine eyes? I am God.

3. Be still, and thou shalt know that I can say to the nations, Peace, be still. The waves rise, but I am mightier than all. These tumults do not touch My throne. Take no alarm because of this world-wide resistance to My authority and law. I am still God.

4. Be still, and thou shalt see the glorious issue of all these confusions. This world is My world, and thou shalt see it to be such; this earth shall yet be the abode of the righteous.—*Bonar.*

Leaves of Gold

WANT.—"The Lord is my shepherd; I shall not want."

I shall not want rest. "He maketh me to lie down in green pastures."

I shall not want drink. "He leadeth me beside the still waters."

I shall not want forgiveness. "He restoreth my soul."

I shall not want guidance. "He leadeth me in the paths of righteousness for His name's sake."

I shall not want companionship. "Yea, though I walk through the valley of the shadow of death, I will fear no evil; for Thou art with me."

I shall not want comfort. "Thy rod and Thy staff they comfort me."

I shall not want food. "Thou preparest a table before me in the presence of mine enemies."

I shall not want joy. "Thou anointest my head with oil."

I shall not want anything. "My cup runneth over."

I shall not want anything in this life. "Surely goodness and mercy shall follow me all the days of my life."

I shall not want anything in eternity. "And I will dwell in the house of the Lord Forever."—*Selected.*

WAIT—Many times, this little verse by Harry Chester has fallen on my heart like a benediction:
The Scripture says that in His own sweet way
    If we but wait,
The Lord will take our burdens and set
    Crooked matters straight.
                    —*Jowett.*

THE STUDY of God's word, for the purpose of discovering God's will, is the secret discipline which has formed the greatest characters.—*J. W. Alexander.*

TEN COMMANDMENTS — Thou shall not have another God but me.

Thou shalt not to an image bow the knee.

Thou shalt not take the Name of God in vain:

See that the Sabbath thou do not profane.

Honor thy father and thy mother too:

In act, or thought, see thou no murder do,

From fornication keep thy body clean:

Thou shalt not steal, though thou be very mean.

Bear no false witness; keep thee without spot,

What is thy neighbor's, see thou covet not.
                    —*John Bunyan.*

BETTER THAN GOLD
O for a Booke and a Shadie Nooke
    Eyther in-a-doore or out;
With the greene leaves whispering over-
        hede,
    Or the Streete cries all aboute,
Where I maie reade all at my ease,
    Bothe of the Newe and Olde,
For a jollie goode Booke whereon to
        looke,
    Is better to me than Golde.
                    —*John Wilson.*

SCHOOL HOURS — The Disciples were not losing time when they sat down beside their Master, and held quiet converse with Him under the olives of Bethany or by the shores of Galilee. Those were their school hours; those were their feeding times. The healthiest Christian, the one who is best fitted for Godly living and Godly labors, is he who feeds most on Christ. Here lies the benefit of Bible reading.—*Evangelist.*

SPIRIT — In Tremont Temple there were two colored men; one of them was Robert. He was born in slavery, never saw the inside of a school, and learned to read only through great effort of his own. But Black Robert knew more about the Bible than any other man in Tremont Temple. Why? I will tell you why. For years Black Robert never read his Bible except on his knees. For two, three, four hours at a time, he read the Bible on his knees. He never went to bed that he did not put the Bible under his pillow, and when they found him dead in a hospital ward they found the Bible under his curly head. I had the privilege of being under one of the great Hebrew scholars of his day. He thought Hebrew, he was saturated in Hebrew; a gentle, Christian man, a great scholar with a great brain. He would come straight to his desk, open that old Hebrew Bible, drop his face right down between the pages, and say something like this: "Oh, Lord Jesus, may thy Holy Spirit teach us the Word." Do you wonder that he knew his Bible? He knew it by the same process that Black Robert knew his. You can't read your Bible without the Holy Spirit.
—*Cortland Myers.*

PSALM XIX—The nineteenth psalm sets forth most beautifully the true relation which ought to exist between God's world and God's word. In the first six verses of that psalm we have natural religion: "The heavens declare the glory of God, and the firmament showeth His handiwork. Day unto day uttereth speech and night unto night showeth knowledge." We have here one of the finest personifications I know of anywhere. One day is represented as calling to the next day, and the next takes up the cry, and passes it on, thus day unto day in cease-

less procession, shows God's wondrous revelation of Himself. In the seventh verse of this psalm you enter into a new atmosphere. You feel now that you are breathing the air more distinctively of Heaven, and that your feet are standing upon the solid rock, for you read, "The law of the Lord is perfect, restoring the soul." Down to the end of the thirteenth verse you have revealed religion and the effect which it produces on action and character. Then in the last verse you have experimental religion: "Let the words of my mouth and the meditations of my heart be acceptable in thy sight, O Lord, my strength and my redeemer." Observe what progress you have in this psalm. You have first, creation; second, revelation; third, generation; natural religion, revealed religion, experimental religion. This psalm is an epitome of the whole Bible.—*Powell.*

GOD'S CHART—The Bible is God's chart for you to steer by, to keep you from the bottom of the sea, and to show you where the harbor is, and how to reach it without running on rocks or bars. If you have been reading it to gratify curiosity; or to see if you could not catch a universalist; or to find a knife with which to cut up a Unitarian; or for the purpose of setting up or taking down a bishop; or to establish or overthrow any sect—if you have been reading it so, then stop. It is God's medicine-book. You are sick. You are mortally struck through with disease. There is no human remedy for your trouble. But here is God's medicine-book. If you read it for life, for growth in righteousness, then blessed is your reading; but if you read it for disputation and dialectical ingenuities, it is no more to you than Bacon's "Novum Organum" would be.—*Beecher.*

Leaves of Gold

OLD TESTAMENT—The Old Testament is the watershed of the New. These deep springs, which irrigate and fructify the New Testament Church, took their rise from the mountains of Judea, and descended, like the volume of the Nile, to fertilize and fructify the landscape around it.—*Gordon.*

ASPECTS OF FAITH — 1. Strong faith will make the soul resolute in resisting, and happy in conquering the strongest temptations.—*Heb.* 11:38; *Dan.* 6:10.

2. It will make a man own God and cleave to, and hang upon God in the face of the greatest difficulties and dangers.—*Psa.* 44:16-18; *Rom.* 4:18.

3. It will enable men to prefer Christ's cross before the world's crown, to prefer tortures before deliverance.—*Heb.* 11:3.

4. It will make a soul divinely fearless, and divinely careless; it will make a man live as a child lives in the family, without fear or care.—*Psa.* 23:4; *Dan.* 3:16; *Micah.* 7:7-9.

5. It will make a man cleave to the promise when Providence runs cross to the promise. — *Numb.* 10:29; *2 Chron.* 20:9-11; *Psa.* 60:6-7.

6. It will make men comply with those commands that do most cross them in their desirable comforts.—*Heb.* 11:8-9.
                                        —*T. Brooks.*

DETERMINATION — The Bible makes much of determination. Choose ye this day whom ye will serve. Strive to enter in at the strait gate. See that ye refuse not Him that speaketh. Quench not the Spirit. Escape for thy life. All this style of admonition and direction shows that the sinner has a host of obstacles between him and Heaven; and he must push his way through, or perish.
                                        —*H. Cuyler.*

GARDEN—The Bible resembles an extensive and highly cultivated flower garden, where there is a vast variety and profusion of fruits and flowers, some of which are more essential or more splendid than others; but there is not a blade suffered to grow in it which has not its use and beauty in the system. Salvation for sinners is the grand truth presented everywhere, and in all points of light; but the pure in heart sees a thousand traits of the Divine character, of himself, and of the world: some striking and bold —others cast as it were into the shade, and designed to be searched for and examined; some direct, others by way of intimation or inference.—*Cecil.*

FARMING

Matt. 21:28: Son, go work today.

Matt. 13:38: The field is the world.

Jer. 4:3: Break up your fallow.

Luke 8:11: The seed is the word of God.

Mark 4:14: The sower soweth the word.

Jer. 4:3: Sow not among thorns.

Eccl. 11:6: In the morning sow.

Prov. 11:18: He that soweth in righteousness.

Ps. 126:5: They that sow in tears.

Eccl. 11:4: He that observeth wind shall not sow.

Ps. 126:6: Bearing precious seed.

Is. 32:20: Blessed are ye that sow.

Hos. 10:12: In righteousness.

2 Cor. 9:6: He that soweth sparingly.

Gal. 6:7: Whatsoever a man soweth.

1 Cor. 3:6: Planted, watered, increase.

Gal. 6:8, 9: He that soweth to the Spirit.

Jno. 4:35: White already to harvest.

Jno. 4:36: He that reapeth receiveth wages.
                                        —*Handy Outlines.*

EPISTLES — In the business world great importance is placed upon letters of recommendation. Yet how worthless such a letter would be if it were illegible! Have you ever seen an illegible letter of recommendation in the Christian life? The Holy Spirit tells us 2 Cor. 3, 3, that we are "epistles of Christ. . . written, not with ink, but with the spirit of the living God." A speaker at America's Keswick in New Jersey said: "Some folks are illegible letters. You can't make out whether they are Christians or not. Their names are on the church record, but so much writing of the world is on them that you can't quite be sure of them."—It is a blessed thing in this day, when Christ is disowned by so many in the visible Church, to have those who will let the Lord Jesus Christ cleanse their hearts from every stain and then permit Him to write plainly and clearly upon their lives that they belong to Him and serve Him.—*The Way.*

TABERNACLE—We may compare the Bible to the Tabernacle with its three courts. The outer court is the letter of the Scripture, the inner court, or holy place, is the truth of the Scripture; the holiest place of all is the person of Jesus Christ; and only when we pass the inmost veil do we come to Him.
—*A. T. Pierson.*

GOOD—A party of engineers became lost in a forest in Africa. Their supply of food was exhausted. They found some berries which seemed to perfectly satisfy the appetite. They ate them for several days, but became weaker and weaker, and one after another died, until, when help came, there was only one left to tell the sad story. They still had some of the berries, but when they were analyzed they were found to be absolutely worthless as a food. While their appetites were satisfied they were actually starving to death. Many people are like that—perfectly satisfied to starve their nature on food which is of no value, while they might feast on the "true bread from Heaven."
—*Miller.*

JOHN 3:16
1. God—the greatest lover.
2. So loved—the greatest degree.
3. The world—the greatest company.
4. That He gave—the greatest act.
5. His only begotten Son—the greatest gift.
6. That whosoever—the greatest opportunity.
7. Believeth—the greatest simplicity.
8. In Him—the greatest attraction.
9. Should not perish—the greatest promise.
10. But—the greatest difference.
11. Have—the greatest certainty.
12. Eternal life—the greatest possession.
—*Davies.*

GUIDE—A man, who was about to take a perilous journey through the mountains, was given not a little advice. As is often the case in such situations, the advice was contradictory. One warned him against taking any of the bypaths that led away from the main road, while others declared that many of these paths could be pursued with profit, since they meant shortening the distance toward his destination. So it was with a number of things that left him in doubt. "It seems," he said to himself, "I shall have to guess at what I do not know." Just then one appeared and said: "I am the authorized guide. I am ready to go with you all the way, if you will but follow my teachings."
—*Mattie M. Boteler.*

EYES OF GOD—All seeing eyes: The eyes of the Lord are in every place, beholding the evil and the good.—Prov. 15:3.

Penetrating eyes: All things are naked and opened unto the eyes of Him with whom we have to do.—Heb. 4:13.

Thoughtful eyes: For the ways of man are before the eyes of the Lord, and He pondereth all His goings.—Prov. 5:21.

Remembering eyes: And they consider not in their hearts that I remember all their wickedness; now their own doings have beset them about; they are before My face.—Hosea 7:2.

Judging eyes: Thine eyes are open upon all the ways of the sons of men; to give every one according to the fruit of his doings.—Jer. 32:19.

Providing eyes: A land which the Lord thy God careth for; the eyes of the Lord thy God are always upon it, from the beginning of the year even unto the end of the year.—Deut. 11:12.

IDENTIFIED—The New Testament scene does not lie in some misty, undefined portion of time, the place of which cannot be ascertained, but in a period as historical and as recognizable as that of Queen Elizabeth or Charles the Second. The geography of the New Testament is historical. It includes empires and kingdoms, provinces and cities, mountains and oceans, rivers and valleys, which are all real and correctly indicated. The smallest villages equally with the largest cities are accurately represented and located. The progress of modern discovery has only tended to confirm the book in its minutest details. This is not usual with mythical and purely fabulous writings, with which, indeed, the rule is quite the opposite.

—B. H. Cowper.

THE STREAM—The Scriptures teach us the best way of living, the noblest way of suffering, and the most comfortable way of dying.—Flavel.

A stream where alike the elephant may swim and the lamb may wade.

—Gregory.

AUTHORS—The Bible itself is a standing and an astonishing miracle. Written, fragment by fragment, throughout the course of fifteen centuries, under different states of society, and in different languages, by persons of the most opposite tempers, talents, and conditions, learned and unlearned, prince and peasant, bond and free; cast into every form of instructive composition and good writing, history, prophecy, poetry, allegory, emblematic representation, judicious interpretation, literal statement, precept, example, proverbs, disquisition, epistle, sermon, prayer—in short all rational shapes of human discourse; and treating, moreover, of subjects not obvious, but most difficult;—its authors are not found, like other writers, contradicting one another upon the most ordinary matters of fact and opinion, but are at harmony upon the whole of their sublime and momentous scheme.—Maclagan.

CONSOLATION — Never on earth calamity so great, as not to leave to us, if rightly weighed, what would console us 'mid what we sorrow for.—Shakespeare.

THE SAVOR LOST — Possession, why more tasteless than pursuit? Why is a wish far dearer than a crown? That wish accomplished, why the grave of bliss? Because, in the great future buried deep, beyond our plans, lies all that man with ardor should pursue.—Young.

IX. COURAGE

SUNSHINE—A Boston daily spoke one day, thus: "The day opened cloudy and cheerless, but about noon Phillips Brooks came down town and then everything brightened up."

Many Christians are just like Phillips Brooks in this respect, and one such Christian is the author of "In the Service of the King." Always he radiated joy and gladness. Early in the first chapter he told how he deliberately made up his mind to do this. One day he was reading Gulliver's tale of the great inventor who had hit upon a device for extracting from cucumbers sunshine which he then "stored away in bottles to be used in the home on dark days to light the house." As he thought on this story "the deacon's mission became clear: he would be the agent of the great inventor, a dispenser of bottled sunshine." So he set out to make his people laugh. "Counting the cost, he deliberately donned the motley . . . With a persistency that even now he feels a pride in, he determined never to desist till he could say that he had had a laugh from every one of his people . . . Whatever else he may have left undone, the deacon knows that in those first days he taught to many a sad heart the long-forgotten trick of laughter. . . Experience gives him courage to insist that when the sunshine is unbottled in the home of desolation, it discovers a heart of gold that was near to perishing in the shadow."

—*John T. Faris.*

FORTITUDE—True fortitude I take to be the quiet possession of a man's self, and an undisturbed doing his duty, whatever evil besets or danger lies in his way.

—*Locke.*

The fortitude of a Christian consists in patience, not in enterprises which the poets call heroic, and which are commonly the effects of interest, pride, and worldly honor.—*Dryden.*

Fortitude implies a firmness and strength of mind, that enables us to do and suffer as we ought. It rises upon an opposition, and, like a river, swells the higher for having its course stopped.

—*Jeremy Collier.*

THE CONQUEST OF FEAR — Courage consists not in hazarding without fear, but being resolutely minded in a just cause. The brave man is not he who feels no fear, for that were stupid and irrational, but he whose noble soul subdues its fear, and bravely dares the danger nature shrinks from.—*Ferrold.*

OPPORTUNITY

*They do me wrong who say I come no
    more
When once I knock and fail to find
    you in;
For every day I stand outside your door,
And bid you wake, and rise to fight
    and win.*

*Wail not for precious chances passed
    away!
Weep not for golden ages on the wane.
Each night I burn the records of the
    day,
At sunrise every soul is born again.*

*Though deep in mire, wring not your
    hands and weep:
I lend my arm to all who say, "I can!"
No shamefaced outcast ever sank so
    deep,
But yet might rise and be again a man!*

—WALTER MALONE.

FAILURE—There are always reasons for giving up. Arguments for self-pity are thick as blackberries. The world is crowded with thorns and cruelties, causes for tears. Courage is the divine unreason against which, as against a rock, the waves of disaster beat in vain. Say to yourself: I am unconquerable. I shall arrive. In the center of creation sits not an enemy, but my Friend. I shall arrive—what time, what circuit first, I ask not. In some time, His good time, I shall arrive. Let come what will, I shall never say I am beaten. I am not a negligible molecule, a mote in the sunbeam, a worm! I am a man, and, so help me God! I shall play the man. Failure! There is no such word in all the bright lexicon of speech, unless you yourself have written it there! There is no such thing as failure except to those who accept and believe in failure.—*Marden.*

MOTIVE POWER—It is only through labor and prayerful effort, by grim energy and resolute courage, that we move on to better things.—*Theodore Roosevelt.*

IGNORANCE—Fear is lack of faith. Lack of faith is ignorance. Fear can only be cured by vision. Give the world eyes. It will see. Give it ears. It will hear. Give it a right arm. It will act. Man needs time and room. Man needs soil, rain and sunshine. Needs a chance. Open all your doors and windows. Let everything pass freely in and out, out and in. Even the evil. Let it pass out and in, in and out. No man hates the truth. But most men are afraid of the truth. Make the truth easier than a lie. Make the truth welcomer than its counterfeits. Then man will no longer be afraid; being afraid is being ignorant. Being ignorant is being without faith.—*Horace Traubel.*

REJOICE—Religion is not a funeral announcement. There are religious leaders who seem to be always saying—"Let us cry." They have gotten the wrong phrase. "Let us rejoice!" When you begin to talk about faith and God, do not turn the corners of your mouth down. Face these matters as naturally, as joyously, as genuinely, as you would face any other interest in life.—*Mills.*

Changed

Time was, I shrank from what was right,
　From fear of what was wrong;
I would not brave the sacred fight,
　Because the foe was strong.
But now I cast that finer sense
　And sorer shame aside;
Such dread of sin was indolence,
　Such aim at Heaven was pride.
　　　　　　　—*J. H. Newman.*

LETTING OUT THE REINS—Every year I live I am more convinced that the waste of life lies in the love we have not given, the powers we have not used, the selfish prudence that will risk nothing, and which, shirking pain, misses happiness as well. No one ever yet was the poorer in the long run for having once in a lifetime "let out all the length of all the reins."
　　　　—*Mary Cholmondeley.*

TAKING CHANCES—No man is worth his salt who is not ready at all times to risk his body, to risk his well-being, to risk his life, in a great cause.
　　　　　—*Theodore Roosevelt.*

WHAT COUNTS—'Tisn't life that matters! It's the courage you bring to it.
　　　　　　—*Hugh Walpole.*

IMPREGNABLE—Courage does not consist in feeling no fear, but in conquering fear. He is the hero who seeing the lions on either side goes straight on, because there his duty lies.

—*Saturday Magazine.*

I hate to see things done by halves. If it be right, do it boldly, if it be wrong, leave it undone.—*Gilpin.*

Courage consists not in hazarding without fear, but being resolutely minded in a just cause.—*Plutarch.*

True courage is the result of reasoning. A brave mind is always impregnable. Resolution lies more in the head than in the veins; and a just sense of honor and of infamy, of duty and of religion, will carry us farther than all the force of mechanism.

—*Jeremy Collier.*

ENVIRONMENT—It is possible to live very near to God under every conceivable environment, and what is possible is our highest duty.

—*William E. McLaren.*

Risky Business

It's a risk to have a husband, a risk to have
  a son;
A risk to pour your confidences out to
  anyone;
A risk to pick a daisy, for there's sure to
  be a cop;
A risk to go on living, but a greater risk
  to stop.

—*Ruth Mason Rice.*

DISCOURAGEMENTS — Pay as little attention to discouragements as possible! Plough ahead as a steamer does, rough or smooth, rain or shine! To carry your cargo and make your port is the point.—*Maltbie Babcock.*

KEEPERS OF THE LIGHT—The keeper of the lighthouse does not launch any ships, it is true, but he keeps many a good ship from going to wreck. The light shines farther than the keeper can see, and brightest when he cannot see at all. Two things he has got to remember—to keep the light burning, and never to get in between the light and the darkness he is set to lighten.—*John T. Faris.*

Steadfast Hearts

Darkness enwrapped him, yet with stead-
  fast heart
  He sought, unfaltering, the highest
    light.
  His keen-eyed spirit failed not in the
    sight
Which sees, and seeing, loves the better
  part.

UNWITNESSED—Perfect valor is to do unwitnessed what we should be capable of doing before all the world.

—*La Rochefoucauld.*

PROTECTION—Though no friend, no man, be with thee, fear nothing! Thy God is here.—*Dinger.*

"Underneath are the everlasting arms." What child of God was ever permitted to fall lower than God's "underneath"?

—*H. Gill.*

Be not faint-hearted in misfortune. When God causes a tree to be hewn down He takes care that His birds can nestle on another.—*Anonymous.*

God accompanies thee, His child—fear not! On each spot that thou standest is an angel of protection; where thou art is thy God; where thy God is there is thy Savior.

THE BRAVEST THING—The Courage we desire and prize is not the Courage to die decently, but to live manfully.
—*Carlyle.*

RESISTANCE — Courage is resistance to fear, mastery of fear—not absence of fear.—*Mark Twain.*

LOST TALENT — A great deal of talent is lost in the world for want of a little courage. Every day sends to their graves obscure men whom timidity prevented from making a first effort; who, if they could have been induced to begin, would in all probability have gone great lengths in the career of fame. The fact is, that to do anything in the world worth doing, we must not stand back shivering and thinking of the cold and danger, but jump in and scramble through as well as we can. It will not do to be perpetually calculating risks and adjusting nice chances; it did very well before the Flood, when a man would consult his friends upon an intended publication for a hundred and fifty years, and live to see his success afterwards; but at present, a man waits, and doubts, and consults his brother, and his particular friends, till one day he finds he is sixty years old and that he has lost so much time in consulting cousins and friends that he has no more time to follow their advice.—*Sydney Smith.*

THE DEBT SIDE—The worst sorrows in life are not in its losses and misfortunes, but its fears.—*A. C. Benson.*

WHAT TO FEAR—Fear not that thy life shall come to an end, but rather fear that it shall never have a beginning.
—*J. H. Newman.*

FREEDOM — Many a boy has discovered that real freedom is never gained by breaking legitimate laws. "Obedience to Law is Liberty" is the appropriate inscription over the massive entrance of a great courthouse in Cleveland, and it is wonderfully true. There is no real liberty in any other course. Just doing what you please, and following that impulse, is not true freedom. Obeying a sudden impulse to follow the primrose path usually starts or strengthens some bad habit which forges shackles on our characters and destroys by just so much our freedom. A lawless person is never free. He is a victim of his own unaccountable impulses and soon a slave to his bad habits.
—*George Walter Fiske.*

THE DIVINE SPARK

Courage—an independent spark from
    heaven's bright throne,
By which the soul stands raised, triumphant, high, alone.
—*George Farquhar.*

HARDSHIP — Dr. Cane, finding a flower under the Humboldt glacier, was more affected by it because it grew beneath the lip and cold bosom of the ice, than he would have been by the most gorgeous garden bloom. So some single struggling grace in the heart of one far removed from Divine influences may be dearer to God than a whole catalog of virtues in the life of one more favored of Heaven.

As in nature, as in art, so in grace; it is rough treatment that gives souls, as well as stones, their lustre. The more the diamond is cut the brighter it sparkles; and in what seems hard dealing, there God has no end in view but to perfect His people.
—*Guthrie.*

X. DEFINITIONS

ADORATION is a universal sentiment: it differs in degree in different natures; it takes the most varied forms,—often ignores its own existence; sometimes it betrays itself by an exclamation uttered from the heart in the midst of the grand scenes of nature and life; sometimes it rises silently in the mute and penetrated soul; it may wander in its mode of expression, and err as to its object.—*V. Cousin.*

THE GREATEST MAN is he who chooses the right with invincible resolution; who resists the sorest temptations from within and without; who bears the heaviest burdens cheerfully; who is calmest in storms, and most fearless under menace and frowns; and whose reliance on truth, on virtue, and on God, is most unfaltering.—*Channing.*

EACH IN HIS OWN TONGUE

A fire-mist and a planet,—
  A crystal and a cell,—
A jellyfish and a saurian,
  And caves where the cavemen dwell;
Then a sense of law and beauty,
  And a face turned from the clod,—
Some call it Evolution,
  And others call it God.

A picket frozen on duty,—
  A mother starved for her brood,—
Socrates drinking the hemlock,
  And Jesus on the rood;
And millions who humble and nameless,
  The straight hard pathway plod,—
Some call it Consecration,
  And others call it God.

—WILLIAM HERBERT CARRUTH.

THE CYNIC is one who never sees a good quality in a man, and never fails to see a bad one.

The *cynic* is one who knows the price of everything and the value of nothing.
—*Oscar Wilde.*

DIFFICULTIES are God's errands; and when we are sent upon them, we should esteem it a proof of God's confidence.—*Beecher.*

GIFTS are what a man has, but graces are what a man is.—*F. W. Robertson.*

SYMPATHY

What is sympathy? It is thinking
More of others than yourself,
Counting hearts of fellow mortals
Of more worth than paltry self,
Acting for your comrade's pleasure,
Giving without stint or art;
It is blessing every creature
With your hand and voice and heart.

ENTHUSIASM is a telescope that yanks the misty, distant future into the radiant, tangible present.

DUTY is a power which rises with us in the morning, and goes to rest with us at night. It is co-extensive with the action of our intelligence. It is the shadow which cleaves to us, go where we will, and which only leaves us when we leave the light of life.—*Gladstone.*

FORTITUDE is the marshal of thought, the armor of the will and the fort of reason.—*Bacon.*

MAN—Every man is a volume, if you know how to read him.—*Channing.*

Flower in the crannied wall,
I pluck you out of the crannies;—
Hold you here, root and all, in my hand,
Little flower—but if I could understand
What you are, root and all, and all in all,
I should know what God and man is.
—*Tennyson.*

PRAYER is a shield to the soul, a sacrifice to God, and a scourge for Satan.
—*Bunyan.*

What Is Good

"What is the real good?"
  I asked in musing mood,
"Order," said the law court;
  "Knowledge," said the school;
"Truth," said the wise man;
  "Pleasure," said the fool;
"Love," said the maiden;
  "Beauty," said the page;
"Freedom," said the dreamer;
  "Home," said the sage;
"Fame," said the soldier;
  "Equity," the seer.
Spake my heart full sadly
  "The answer is not here."
Then within my bosom
  Softly this I heard:
"Each heart holds the secret,
  Kindness is the word."
—*John Boyle O'Reilly.*

FRIENDSHIP is, strictly speaking, reciprocal benevolence, which inclines each party to be solicitous for the welfare of the other as for his own. This equality of affection is created and preserved by a similarity of disposition and manners.—*Plato.*

HELL is truth seen too late.—*Adam.*

FAITH is the soul riding at anchor.
—*H. W. Shaw.*

PERSEVERENCE is failing nineteen times and succeeding the twentieth.
—*J. Andrews.*

RICHES—To have what we want is riches, but to be able to do without is power.—*Donald Grant.*

STATEMANSHIP — True statesmanship consists of discovering which way God is going and getting the obstacles out of the way.—*Gunsaulus.*

ADVERSITY is the path of truth.
—*Byron.*

CHRISTIANITY is a battle, not a dream.—*Wendell Phillips.*

SAINT—"A little child on a summer morning stood in a great Cathedral Church. The sunlight streamed through the beautiful stained glass windows and the figures in them of the servants of God were bright with brilliant color. A little later the question was asked, 'What is a saint?' and the child replied, A saint is a person who lets the light shine through'."—*Anonymous.*

GOD—That unity of bests.
—*Mrs. Browning.*

PREACHERS—"The poorest of trades and the noblest of callings," is what Dr. Cuyler calls the ministry of the Gospel.

PRUDENCE is the footprint of wisdom.—*A. Bronson Alcott.*

Leaves of Gold

XI. EDUCATION

INFLUENCE — James A. Garfield said that a log with a student on one end and Mark Hopkins, his old teacher, on the other end was his ideal college. The point in it all is that personal contact and direct interest in the individual student by an instructor of lofty character is the main thing in any institution of learning.—*F. S. Groner.*

TRUTH — Nobody wants mathematics from a Methodist viewpoint, nor physics as a Presbyterian doctrine, nor chemistry as a Congregational subject, nor ethics from an Episcopalian angle, nor dogma mixed with science, nor denominationalism taught. But with its chief and eternal concern with truth, the Church is becoming free intellectually and spiritually through truth wherever discovered.
—*Winifred Willard.*

THE THINKER

Back of the beating hammer
  By which the steel is wrought,
Back of the workshop's clamor
  The seeker may find the thought;
The thought that is ever master
  Of iron and steam and steel,
That rises above disaster
  And tramples it under heel!

Might of the roaring boiler,
  Force of the engine's thrust,
Strength of the sweating toiler,
  Greatly in these we trust.
But back of them stands the schemer,
  The thinker who drives things
    through;
Back of the job—the dreamer,
  Who's making the dream come true!
—BERTON BRALEY.
Copyright by Berton Braley, all rights reserved.

INSPIRATION — I read in Shakespeare of the majesty of the moral law, in Victor Hugo the sacredness of childhood, in Tennyson, the ugliness of hypocrisy, in George Elliot the supremacy of duty, in Dickens the divinity of kindness, and in Ruskin the dignity of service. Irving teaches me the lesson of cheerfulness. Hawthorne shows me the hatefulness of sin, Longfellow gives me the soft, tranquil music of hope. Lowell makes us feel that we must give ourselves to our fellow men. Whittier sings to me of divine Fatherhood and human brotherhood. These are Christian lessons. Who inspired them?

Who put it into the heart of Martin Luther to nail those theses on the church door of Wittenberg? Who stirred and fired the soul of Savonarola? Who thrilled and electrified the soul of John Wesley? Jesus Christ is back of these all.
—*Powell.*

SCIENCE—The goal of science is to describe the universe; the goal of religion is to find the most abundant life which man may possess in such a universe.
—*Kirtley F. Mather.*

RELIGION as regards its general influence over the mind of a nation, apart from and independent of religious education, forms a separate and very important element in the promotion of civilization. The Christian religion is in its nature highly favorable to the civilization alike of individuals and of states, and both intellectually and morally. The knowledge that it teaches is the highest and most elevating; and the principles that it enforces are the purest and most comprehensive.—*George Harris.*

58

THE WAY TO FREEDOM — We are accustomed to say that the truth makes men free. It does nothing of the kind. It is the knowledge of the truth that creates freedom. "Ye shall know the truth, and the truth shall make you free." We are now at the stage where the main emphasis must be laid on the dissemination of the truth. We need as we have never needed a campaign of education, with men and women going hither and thither in a great lecture campaign, weaving itself across this nation like a weaver's shuttle. We need a baptism of the right kind of literature, periodicals, and truth-carrying messages that will make the people of the nations and the rest of the world sit up and take notice. We have reached the place where we can no longer take the defensive; we must once again resume the offensive. The colleges, universities, and high schools, with the three millions of young men and women in those institutions, who are to take their place in the life of the nation just a few years hence, are the laboratory where truth must be demonstrated.

—*Ernest H. Cherrington.*

STAGNANT TRUTH—Do not mistake acquirement of mere knowledge for power. Like food, these things must be digested and assimilated to become life or force. Learning is not wisdom; knowledge is not necessarily vital energy. The student who has to cram through a school or a college course, who has made himself merely a receptacle for the teacher's thoughts and ideas, is not educated; he has not gained much. He is a reservoir, not a fountain. One retains, the other gives forth. Unless his knowledge is converted into wisdom, into faculty, it will become stagnant like still water.

—*J. E. Dinger.*

HEAD VS. HEART—What I am concerned about in this fast-moving world in a time of crisis, both in foreign and domestic affairs, is not so much a program as a spirit of approach, not so much a mind as a heart. A program lives today and dies tomorrow. A mind, if it be open, may change with each day, but the spirit and the heart are as unchanging as the tides.

—*Owen D. Young.*

A builder builded a temple;
  He wrought with care and skill;—
Pillars and groins and arches
  Were fashioned to meet his will;
And men said when they saw its beauty:
  "It shall never know decay.
Great is thy skill, O Builder,
  Thy fame shall endure for aye."

A teacher builded a temple;
  She wrought with skill and care;—
Forming each pillar with patience,
  Laying each stone with prayer.
None saw the unceasing effort;
  None knew of the marvelous plan;
For the temple the teacher builded
  Was unseen by the eyes of man.

Gone is the builder's temple;—
  Crumbled into the dust,—
Pillar and groin and arches
  Food for consuming rust;
But the temple the teacher builded
  Shall endure while the ages roll;—
For that beautiful, unseen temple
  Was a child's immortal soul.

REFLECTION — The man who thinks, reads, studies, and meditates has intelligence cut in his features, stamped on his brow, gleaming in his eyes, and sooner or later the face tells the status or the condition of the soul—a reflection of the divinity within the man.—*Record.*

STUDY—A beginning of days to many preachers would be to take possession of some new province of literature, as Robert Hall did when, after sixty, he studied Italian to read Dante; as Arnold did when, two years before his death, he began Sanskrit, pleading that he "was not so old as Cato when he learned Greek." How many weary and starved congregations listen hopelessly to a dejected preacher who will never give them a word, a phrase, or a thought they have not heard hundreds of times.—*Beecher.*

DEDICATION—Let us now with earnest hearts and with exalted faith and hope solemnly consecrate this building to its high and holy purpose. May the youth of this community for generations to come gather in this place to receive instruction in knowledge and training in virtue. May they find here every condition necessary to a true and enlightened education. Especially, may their teachers be examples of excellence in scholarship and character, seekers after goodness and truth, lovers of children, enthusiasts and adepts in the finest of all arts, the development and inspiration of human souls. May these rooms always be pervaded with an invigorating atmosphere of mental and moral life, and may no child pass from these schools to higher grades or to the outer world without having been made more intelligent, more thoughtful, more courageous, more virtuous, and in every way more capable of wise and just, of useful and noble living. To this end, may the blessing of God be upon child and parent, upon pupil and teacher, upon principal and superintendent and upon every one whose influence will in any degree affect the work of education as it shall be conducted within these walls.
—*Scott.*

EXPERIENCE TEACHES—It is not enough to have books, or to know where to read up for information when we want it. Practical wisdom for the purposes of life must be carried about with us, and be ready for use at call. It is not enough that we have a fund laid up at home, but not a farthing in our pocket: we must carry about with us a store of the current coin of knowledge ready for exchange on all occasions, else we are helpless when the opportunity for action occurs. The experience gathered from books is of the nature of learning; the experience gained from actual life is of the nature of wisdom; and a small store of the latter is worth vastly more than any stock of the former.
—*Smiles.*

THE TEACHER

Lord, who am I to teach the way
    To little children day by day,
So prone myself to go astray?

I teach them knowledge, but I know
    How faint they flicker and how low
The candles of my knowledge glow.

I teach them power to will and do,
    But only now to learn anew
My own great weakness thru and thru.

I teach them love for all mankind
    And all God's creatures, but I find
My love comes lagging far behind.

Lord, if their guide I still must be,
    Oh, let the little children see
The teacher leaning hard on Thee.
—*Leslie Pinckney Hill.*

TRUE REPOSE—I have sought repose everywhere, and I have found it only in a little corner with a little book.
—*St. Francois de Sales.*

Leaves of Gold

RIGHTEOUSNESS—President Mc-Cosh, in his Baccalaureate sermon, said to the graduating boys: "I say to you intending lawyers, see that ye yield to no crookedness; and to you intending merchants, that ye be honorable in all your transactions; to you intending journalists, that ye write only what ye know to be true; and you, ministers of the everlasting Gospel, that your aim be to win souls to Christ; and to all that ye live soberly, righteously, and godly."

THE ART OF LIVING WELL — "Public instruction," said Napoleon, "should be the first object of government." "All who have meditated on the art of governing mankind," said Aristotle, "have been convinced that the fate of empires depends upon the education of youth." "Knowledge," said Daniel Webster, "does not comprise all which is contained in the large term 'education'. The feelings are to be disciplined, the passions are to be restrained, true and worthy motives are to be instilled, and pure morality inculcated under all circumstances. All this is comprised in education." "Teach," said Seneca, "the art of living well." "Reason and experience both forbid us to expect," said Washington, "that national morality can prevail in exclusion of religious principles." "Educate men without religion," said the Duke of Wellington, "and you make of them but clever devils." "Religion and liberty are inseparable," said Philip Schaff. "True religion," said Burke, "is the foundation of society. When that is once shaken by contempt the whole fabric cannot be stable or lasting."—Public Speakers Library.

FUNDAMENTALS—Manhood, not scholarship, is the first aim of education.
—Ernest Thompson Seton.

A NATION'S DESTINY—A nation's destiny is not in its learning or the amount of information it acquires—it's in its character. The heart of culture is the culture of the heart. The only way to form character is through religion. Find me another way and I'll accept it. The only system of education worthy of the name of system, much less education, is that one which literally and actually inculcates the eternal truth of morality, not only by teaching, but by hour-to-hour example. I do not speak as a politician. I am speaking as an expert. I am not a theorist. The reason I dare speak is that every day, every hour, I am face to face with the real thing here, with the facts.
—Talley.

SHAMS—As one grows older one is more impatient with subterfuges and shams generally, and increasingly desirous that the "last run" at least should be free from them. The world is apparently so confused that the least one can do for it is to keep one's mental integrity and to hold honestly to such poor wisdom as one has been able to garner on the way.
—Jane Addams.

EXAMPLE—Education does not mean teaching people what they do not know. It means teaching them to behave as they do not behave. It is not teaching the youth the shapes of letters and the tricks of numbers, and then leaving them to turn their arithmetic to roguery, and their literature to lust. It means, on the contrary, training them into the perfect exercise and kingly continence of their bodies and souls. It is a painful, continual and difficult work to be done by kindness, by watching, by warning, by precept, and by praise, but above all—by example.
—John Ruskin.

HUMAN SCULPTURE—A statue lies hid in a block of marble, and the art of statuary only clears away the superfluous matter and removes the rubbish. The figure is in the stone; the sculpture only finds it. What sculpture is to a block of marble, education is to a human soul. The philosopher, the saint, or the hero, the wise, the good or the great man, very often lies hid and concealed in a plebian, which a proper education might have disinterred, and have brought to light.

—Addison.

WISDOM—A man should never be ashamed to own he has been in the wrong, which is but saying in other words that he is wiser today than he was yesterday.

—Pope.

STUDYING—I would say to every person read with your pencil. Never pass a word, or an allusion, or a name you do not understand without marking it down for inquiry. Then go to your dictionary for the definition or explanation; go to the encyclopedia for information as to biographical or historical allusions. Never read about any country without having a map before you. This kind of study will fix things in your minds as no formal method of the schools ever will.

—Beecher.

READ the best books first, or you may not have a chance to read them at all.

—Thoreau.

SAFETY FIRST—The safety of our sons and daughters as they go out on the streets this very night is due to the influence of the preachers rather than to policemen and lawmakers. The safety of our nation, including all groups, depends on Christian education.—Roger Babson.

INTELLECT—The intellect makes religion a science; the heart feels it as a life. To the one it is philosophy; to the other, practice. The one cannot, by its very nature, find what it seeks; the other cannot miss it. Mere intellect can only see the trailing garments of God as He passes by; love lies in His bosom. Tasking himself beyond his powers, man is lost when he seeks to think out the Infinite. As a phantom is said to rise in the desert and beckon the traveler into its depths to perish, speculation tempts the mind into the trackless wastes of the unknown, to lose itself in immensity. True wisdom comes in the end to feel, with Socrates, that the highest knowledge is to know that we know nothing.—Selected.

Church

What is the church? The church is man
  when his awed soul goes out,
In reverence to a mystery that swathes
  him all about.
When any living man in awe gropes
  Godward in his search;
Then in that hour, that living man becomes the living church,
Then, though in wilderness or in waste,
  his soul is swept along
Down naves of prayer, through aisles of
  praise, up altar-stairs of song.
And where man fronts the Mystery with
  spirit bowed in prayer,
There is the universal church—the church
  of God is there.

From SONGS OF THE AVERAGE MAN. By Sam Walter Foss. Copyright 1907, Lothrop, Lee & Shepard Co., Inc., New York.

LEADERS — We are building many splendid churches in this country, but we are not providing leaders to run them. I would rather have a wooden church with a splendid parson than a splendid church with a wooden parson.—Drury.

ONE-SIDED.—I distrust the man of one book, or of one class of books. A lawyer may get no direct aid from Tennyson, but you may more safely trust your case with him, because the fact of reading such an author indicates that he covers more space in human thought. A physician cannot study human nature in Shakespeare without getting a conception of man helpful in his practice. Nor will a preacher be any the worse, but all the better, for not confining himself to works of theology. The men who think and read in various directions are the better entitled to their opinions. Read variously, and you will find after a time that one of the chief delights of reading is substantiating what you find in one department by what you find in another. One thus follows the hidden threads which bind the creation into a unity.—*T. T. Munger.*

WHO IS EDUCATED?—A professor in Chicago is reported to have given the following test to his pupils. He told them they were not really educated unless they could say Yes to all these questions:

Has your education given you sympathy with all good causes and made you espouse them?

Has it made you public-spirited?

Has it made you a brother to the weak?

Have you learned how to make friends and to keep them?

Do you know what it is to be a friend yourself?

Can you look an honest man or a pure woman straight in the eye?

Do you see anything to love in a little child?

Will a lonely dog follow you down the street?

Can you be high-minded and happy in the meaner drudgeries of life?

Do you think washing dishes and hoeing corn just as compatible with high thinking as piano playing or golf?

Are you good for anything to yourself? Can you be happy alone?

Can you look out on the world and see anything but dollars and cents?

Can you look into a mud puddle by the wayside and see anything in the puddle but mud?

Can you look into the sky at night and see beyond the stars?

Can your soul claim relationship with the Creator?

A GREAT MAN is what he is, because he was what he was.

To a Music Teacher

You cannot practice for her every day
The knowledge that you give her will not
    stream
On her young mind in one bright, blind-
    ing ray
But you can plant a dream.

Ah, you can plant a dream in her young
    heart
A dream of excellence whose light will
    gleam
Upon her pathway as the years depart
Your words can plant a dream.

To sow a dream and see it spread and
    grow
To light a lamp and watch its brightness
    gleam
Here is a gift that is divine I know
To give a child a dream.
          —*Anne Campbell.*

INSURANCE.—"Cultivate literature and useful knowledge, for the purpose of qualifying the rising generation for patrons of good government, virtue and happiness."—*George Washington.*

XII. FAITH

BELIEF—An Every-Day Creed—I *believe* in my job. It may not be a very important job, but it is *mine*. Furthermore, it is God's job, for *me*. He has a purpose in my life with reference to His plan for the world's progress. No other fellow can take my place. It isn't a big place, to be sure, but for years I have been molded in a peculiar way to fill a peculiar niche in the world's work. I could take no other man's place. He has the same claim as a specialist that I make for myself. In the end the man whose name was never heard beyond the house in which he lived, or the shop in which he worked, may have a larger place than the chap whose name has been a household word in two continents. Yes, I believe in my job. May it be kept true to the task which lies before me—true to myself and to God, who intrusted me with it.

I *believe* in my fellow-man. He may not always agree with me. I'd feel sorry for him if he did, because I myself do not believe some of the things that were absolutely sure in my own mind a dozen years ago. May he never lose faith in himself, because, if he does, he may lose faith in me, and that would hurt him more than the former, and it would really hurt him more than it would hurt me.

I *believe* in my country. I believe in it because it is made up of my fellow-men —and myself. I can't go back on either of us and be true to my creed. If it isn't the best country in the world it is partly because I am not the kind of a man that I should be.

I *believe* in my home. It isn't a rich home. It wouldn't satisfy some folks, but it contains jewels which cannot be purchased in the markets of the world. When I enter its secret chambers, and shut out the world with its care, I am a lord. Its motto is Service, its reward is Love. There is no other spot in all the world which fills its place, and heaven can be only a larger home, with a Father who is all-wise and patient and tender.

I *believe* in today. It is all that I possess. The past is of value only as it can make the life of today fuller and freer. There is no assurance of tomorrow. I must make good today!—*Charles Stelzle.*

O world, thou choosest not the better
    part!
It is not wisdom to be only wise,
And on the inward vision close the
    eyes,
But it is wisdom to believe the heart.
Columbus found a world and had no
    chart,
Save one that faith deciphered in the
    skies;
To trust the soul's invincible surmise
Was all his science and his only art.
Our knowledge is a torch of smoky pine
That lights the pathway but one step
    ahead
Across a void of mystery and dread.
Bid, then, the tender light of faith to
    shine
By which alone the mortal heart is led
Unto the thinking of the thought di-
    vine.

—GEORGE SANTAYANA.

GREAT ERAS—All great ages have been ages of belief. I mean, when there was any extraordinary power of performance, when great national movements began, when arts appeared, when heroes existed, when poems were made, the human soul was in earnest.

—*Ralph Waldo Emerson.*

AS A MAN THINKETH—A competent scientist reports the result of a test with three men in the British Army: "I asked the three men to submit themselves to a test designed to measure the effect of their mental attitude on their physical strength, this strength to be registered by a single gripping device operated by the right hand. In their normal state, these three men had an average grip of 101 pounds. When, under hypnosis, I told them they were very weak, their utmost effort registered only 29 pounds. But when, still keeping the men under hypnosis, I told them they were very strong, their average strength jumped back to the normal 101 pounds and then rose to 142 pounds. They were actually 40% stronger when they believed they were strong, and actually 70% weaker when they believed they were weak."

IN SPITE OF DUNGEON, FIRE, OR SWORD
I have loved justice; therefore have I borne
Conflict and labor, plot and biting scorn.
Guardian of Faith, for Christ's dear sake
　　would I
Suffer with gladness and in prison die.
　　　　　　　　—Pope Leo XIII.

IMPOSSIBILITIES—Faith laughs at impossibilities, and says "it shall be done." Abraham's faith was adventurous when he went out, not knowing whither he went. Every promise claimed is a promice possessed. Believe, and thou shalt see. Those who are afraid of the deep will not catch many fishes. Have the courage to "launch out." We need pioneers in the realms of faith as well as in the dark places of the earth, and no other field of exploration can ever yield such rewards, for "every place where the sole of your feet shall tread upon shall be yours."
　　　　　　　　—S. S. Times.

BEYOND THE FACTS—There need not be in religion, or music, or art, or love, or goodness, anything that is against reason; but never while the sun shines will we get great religion, or music, or art, or love, or goodness, without going beyond reason.
　　　　　　—Harry Emerson Fosdick.

QUIETNESS

"Be still and know that I am God,"
That I who made and gave thee life
Will lead thy faltering steps aright;
That I who see each sparrow's fall
Will hear and heed thy earnest call.
　　I am God.

"Be still and know that I am God,"
When aching burdens crush thy heart,
Then know I form thee for thy part
And purpose in the plan I hold.
　　Trust in God.

"Be still and know that I am God,"
Who made the atom's tiny span
And set it moving to My plan,
That I who guide the stars above
Will guide and keep thee in My love.
　　Be thou still.
　　　　　　　　—Doran.

IMPROVING—Such as do not grow in grace, decay in grace. There is no standing at a stay in religion, either we go forward or backward; if faith does not grow, unbelief will; if heavenly mindedness doth not grow, covetousness will. A man that doth not increase his stock diminisheth it; if you do not improve your stock of grace, your stock will decay. The angels on Jacob's ladder were either ascending or descending; if you do not ascend in religion, you descend.
　　　　　　　　—T. Watson.

HOPE!—Who is insensible to the music of that word? What bosom has not kindled under its utterance? Poetry has sung of it; music has warbled it; oratory has lavished on it its bewitching strains. Fled from the world, Hope, with her elastic dreams, said that when all other divinities fled from the world, Hope, with her elastic step and radiant countenance and lustrous attire, lingered behind. Hope! well may we personify thee, lighting up thy altar-fires in this dark world, and dropping a live coal into many desolate hearts; gladdening the sick chamber with visions of returning health; illuminating with rays, brighter than the sunbeam, the captive's cell; crowding the broken slumbers of the soldier by his bivouac-fire with pictures of his sunny home and his own joyous return. Hope! drying the tear on the cheek of woe! As the black clouds of sorrow break and fall to the earth, arching the descending drops with thine own beauteous rainbow! Ay, more, standing with thy lamp in thy hand by the gloomy realms of Hades, kindling thy torch at Nature's funeral pile, and opening vistas through the gates of glory! If Hope, even with reference to present and infinite things, be an emotion so joyous—if uninspired poetry can sing so sweetly of its delights, what must be the believer's hope, the hope which has God for its object and Heaven its consummation?

—*John MacDuff.*

God's Witnesses

I need not shout my faith. Thrice eloquent
　Are quiet trees and the green listening
　　sod;
Hushed are the stars, whose power is
　never spent;
　The hills are mute: yet how they speak
　　of God!

—*Charles Hanson Towne.*

FAITH and obedience are bound up in the same bundle. He that obeys God trusts God; and he that trusts God obeys God. He that is without faith is without works; and he that is without works is without faith.—*Spurgeon.*

His Strength

And, as the path of duty is made plain,
May grace be given that I may walk there-
　in,
　Not like the hireling, for his selfish gain,
With backward glances and reluctant
　tread,
Making a merit of his coward dread,—
　But, cheerful, in the light around me
　　thrown,
　Walking as one to pleasant service led;
　Doing God's will as if it were my own,
Yet trusting not in mine, but in His
　strength alone!

—*John Greenleaf Whittier.*

LIFT THE LATCH—Israel could not enter Canaan because of their unbelief. There is many a promised land from which we are excluded for the same reason. For instance, how many of us enjoy the "perfect peace" which is the privilege of the true believer? How many of us have got beyond "hoping" we are saved and "trusting" we are forgiven? They which have believed "do enter into rest." But this Canaan is denied to the only half-believer. He is like a foolish child lingering on a cold, wintry, tempestuous night out in the snow and the wind, while all is warm and tranquil at the fireside within—the supper spread for him, and a vacant seat placed at the table ready for him—because he cannot bring himself fully to believe that if he lifted the latch he would receive instant and joyful welcome.

—*J. Halsey.*

EQUATIONS — Two and two make four—that is mathematics; hydrogen and oxygen form water—that is chemistry; Christ crucified is the power of God unto salvation—that is revelation. But how do you know? Put two and two together and you have four: count and see. Put hydrogen and oxygen together and you have water: test and you will prove it. Believe in the Lord Jesus Christ and thou shalt be saved: believe and you will know. Each demonstration is unanswerable in its own sphere.

—F. G. Penticost.

WAITING

Serene, I fold my hands and wait,
Nor care for wind, nor tide, nor sea;
I rave no more 'gainst time or fate,
For, lo! mine own shall come to me.

I stay my haste, I make delays,
For what avails this eager pace?
I stand amid the eternal ways,
And what is mine shall know my face.

Asleep, awake, by night or day,
The friends I seek are seeking me;
No wind can drive my bark astray,
Nor change the tide of destiny.

What matter if I stand alone?
I wait with joy the coming years;
My heart shall reap where it has sown,
And garner up its fruit of tears.

The waters know their own, and draw
The brook that springs in yonder
heights;
So flows the good with equal law
Unto the soul of pure delights.

The stars come nightly to the sky;
The tidal wave comes to the sea;
Nor time, nor space, nor deep, nor high,
Can keep my own away from me.

—John Burroughs.

REVERENCE — In England, as in America, audiences uniformly rise when choirs begin to sing the Hallelujah Chorus in the Oratorio of the Messiah. In Albert Hall, London, a great audience was assembled. Victoria, the Great and the Good, was present in the royal box. The audience rose, but the noble queen remained seated. Soon every eye was directed to the royal box in which sat the queen. On rolled the magnificent chorus; but the queen remained seated. Higher still rose the lofty song; onward swept the glorious music. With curious glances, the audience turned to the royal box in which the queen remained seated. Loftier still rose the celestial notes. Now the song reached the part where Christ is praised as "King of kings and Lord of lords." The swelling song puts the crown of universal dominion on His divine brow. Then the noble queen arose and stood with bowed head, as if she would cast the crown of her mighty empire at the pierced feet of her divine Lord. Creation and revelation, art and science, song and story, learning and genius, and all earthly rulers reach their noblest heights when they bend in lowliest reverence at the feet of Jesus Christ.—McArthur.

THE EVIDENCE

In every seed to breathe the flower,
In every drop of dew
To reverence a cloistered star
Within the distant blue;
To wait the promise of the bow
Despite the cloud between,
Is Faith—the fervid evidence
Of loveliness unseen.

—John B. Tabb.

OPINIONS—A string of opinions no more constitutes faith, than a string of beads constitutes holiness.—J. Wesley.

EVIDENCE—Thousands and tens of thousands have gone through the evidence which attests the resurrection of Christ, piece by piece, as carefully as ever a judge summed up on the most important case. I have myself done it many times over, not to persuade others, but to satisfy myself. I have been used for many years to study the history of other times, and to examine and weigh the evidence of those who have written about them, and I know of no fact in the history of mankind which is proved by better and fitter evidence and every kind.—*Arnold.*

ATTAINMENT

Use all your hidden forces. Do not miss
The purpose of this life, and do not wait
For circumstance to mold or change your
    fate.
In your own self lies destiny. Let this
Vast truth cast out all fear, all prejudice,
All hesitation. Know that you are great,
Great with divinity. So dominate
Environment, and enter into bliss.—
Love largely and hate nothing. Hold no
    aim
That does not chord with universal good.
Hear what the voices of the silence say,
'All joys are yours if you put forth your
    claim,
Once let the spiritual laws be understood,
Material things must answer and obey.
    —*Ella Wheeler Wilcox.*

THE OLD-TIME RELIGION —
Someone has said, "If we could get religion like a Baptist, experience it like a Methodist, be positive about it like a Disciple, be proud of it like an Episcopalian, pay for it like a Presbyterian, propagate it like an Adventist, and enjoy it like a Negro—that would be some religion!"
    —*Harry Emerson Fosdick.*

GREATEST — My greatest loss — To lose my soul.

My greatest gain—Christ my Savior.

My greatest object—To glorify God.

My greatest pride—A crown of glory.

My greatest work—To win souls for Christ.

My greatest joy—The joy of God's salvation.

My greatest inheritance—Heaven and its glories.

My greatest victory — Over death through Christ.

My greatest neglect—To neglect so great salvation.

My greatest crime—To reject Christ the only Savior.

My greatest privilege — Power to become a son of God.

My greatest bargain—The loss of all things to win Christ.

My greatest profit—Godliness in this life and that to come.

My greatest peace — That peace that passeth understanding.

My greatest knowledge—To know God and Jesus Christ whom He hath sent.
    —*Dinger.*

MY CREED

I would be true, for there are those that
    trust me;
  I would be pure, for there are those who
    care;
I would be strong, for there is much to
    suffer;
I would be brave, for there is much to
    dare.
I would be friend of all — the foe — the
    friendless;
  I would be giving, and forget the gift;
I would be humble, for I know my weak-
    ness;
  I would look up—and laugh—and love
    —and lift.
    —*Howard Arnold Walter.*

MOTIVE POWER—Roger W. Babson says: "A man's religion may be strengthened by connection with a live church. But your religion must be part of you, something you feel in your heart and practise in your life." Then he adds: "Religion changes a human being from a small ineffective detached unit, into a part of a mighty whole. It makes him serve others, and this service is returned to him in kind."

There Is No Unbelief

There is no unbelief;
Whoever plants a seed beneath the sod
And waits to see it push away the clod—
  He trusts in God.

There is no unbelief;
Whoever says when clouds are in the sky,
"Be patient, heart; light breaketh by and
  by,"
Trusts the Most High.

There is no unbelief;
Whoever sees 'neath winter's field of
  snow,
The silent harvest of the future grow—
  God's power must know.

There is no unbelief;
Whoever says "tomorrow," "the un-
  known,"
"The future," trusts the power alone
  He dares disown.

There is no unbelief;
The heart that looks on when the eyelids
  close,
And dares to live when life has only woes,
  God's comfort knows.

There is no unbelief;
For thus by day and night unconsciously
The heart lives by that faith the lips deny.
  God knoweth why!
          —Elizabeth York Case.

THE STAR — Christ is our star of Hope. I want my death-bed to be under that star. All other light will fail. The light that falls from the scroll of fame, the light that flashes from the gem in the beautiful apparel, the light that flashes from the lamps of a banquet—but this light burns on and on. Paul kept his eye on that star until he could say, "I have finished my course." Edward Payson kept his eye on that star until he could say, "The breezes of Heaven fan my brow." John Tennant kept his eye on that star until he could say, "Welcome Lord Jesus, welcome eternity." No other star ever pointed a man into so safe a harbor.
          —Talmage.

Trust

Build a little fence of trust
  Around today;
Fill each space with loving work
  And therein stay;
Look not through the sheltering bars
  Upon tomorrow,
God will help thee bear what comes,
  Of joy or sorrow.
          —Mary Frances Butts.

EXPERT ADVICE—It is the testimony of people who have tried Christianity. Whenever we wish to know anything we go to one who knows. We seek an expert. If we wish to know something about bridges, we go to a bridge builder. If it be medicine, we go to a physician; law, to a lawyer; agriculture, to a specialist in that department. Why not follow the same rule in religious investigations? Instead of asking an agnostic, whose boast is that he knows nothing about Christianity, let us have the testimony of one who has tried it and who out of his personal experience can say: "I know Whom I have believed."—Vance.

NO EASY WAY — There are very few things in this world worth having which can be had cheaply. What we have come to call the strenuous life is essential to all acquisition. One can not get his living for the asking; he must work for his living. Why should it require less persistency and alertness to find a God than is necessary to find a dollar? I once heard a young man remark that the name of God had lost to him all significance. When, however, he was asked whether his interests, reading, and companionships had been such as to keep the spiritual life real and near, he was frank enough to answer that he had never given a thought to such matters for years. He had been living in quite another world, but he fancied that if religion were real, it would somehow break into his world by force. — *Francis G. Peabody.*

DEPENDENCE ON GOD
Lord, I am like to mistletoe,
Which has no root and cannot grow
Or prosper, but by that same tree
It clings about; so I by Thee.
What need I then to fear at all
So long as I about Thee crawl?
But if that tree should fall and die,
Tumble shall Heaven, and so down will I.
　　　　　　　—*Robert Herrick.*

REVERENCE — The most striking fact in modern life is the growing reverence for the teachings and character of Jesus Christ. As once his brothers' sheaves bowed down before Joseph's sheaf, so today art, literature, law, trade, reform, manifest more and more reverence for that Divine Teacher whose sublime figure already fills the whole horizon, and whose teachings are founded as surely as the mountains and stars.
　　　　　　　—*Newell Dwight Hillis.*

THE SILVER CORD — Faith is the silver thread upon which the pearls of the graces are to be strung. Break that, and you have broken the string — the pearls lie scattered on the ground; nor can you wear them for your own adornment. Faith is the mother of virtues. Faith is the fire which consumes sacrifice. Faith is the water which nurtures the root of piety. If you have not faith, all your graces must die. And in proportion as your faith increases, so will all your virtues be strengthened, not all in the same proportion, but all in some degree. — *C. H. Spurgeon.*

SUPPORT — Dr. Griffith Thomas told of the long-time search of the great missionary John G. Paton for a word to use for faith, or belief, when he was making a translation of the Scriptures into the language of those to whom he was seeking to bring Christ. Apparently there was no native word for "believe." For a long time Dr. Paton was well nigh baffled. One day, while working on the translation, a native came into his study, and, tired out, flung himself down on a chair, rested his feet on another chair, and lay back full length, saying as he did so something about how good it was to lean his whole weight on those chairs. Instantly Dr. Paton noted the word the man had used for "lean his whole weight on." The missionary had his word for "believe!" He used it once, and thereafter, in translating the Scriptures. Try it for yourself and see, in any verse that uses the word "believe." "For God so loved the world, that he gave his only begotten Son, that whosoever leans his whole weight on him should not perish, but have eternal life." (John 3:16.) "What must I do to be saved? . . . Lean thy whole weight on the Lord Jesus, and thou shalt be saved." (Acts 16:30, 31.) — *S. S. Times.*

HERITAGE—Paul is yours to lay, as a wise master-builder, the foundation of your faith. Apollos is yours to build on that foundation, to enrich you with his learning, and inspire you with his eloquence. Cephas is yours, with his impetuous devotion, and his stirring reminiscences, and his zeal and experience; all that these have, and all that they are, all that in them can minister to your growth in grace are made over to you. Every variety of Christian sentiment and character is yours if you are Christians at all. You, as joint-heirs with Christ, have a vested right in them which can never be taken away. You, though to the eye of man you may have nothing, in truth possess all things.—*Duckworth.*

The Monitor

A curious child, who dwelt upon a tract
Of inland ground, applying to his ear
The convolutions of a smooth-lipped shell;
To which, in silence hushed, his very soul
Listened intensely; and his countenance
    soon
Brightened with joy; for murmurings from
    within
Were heard, sonorous cadences! whereby
To his belief, the monitor expressed
Mysterious union with his native sea.
Even in such a shell the Universe itself
Is to the ear of Faith: and there are times,
I doubt not, when to you it doth impart
Authentic tidings of invisible things;
Of ebb and flow and ever-during power;
And central peace, subsisting at the heart
Of endless agitation.
    —*William Wordsworth.*

DOUBTS—I will listen to any one's convictions, but pray keep your doubts to yourself.—*Goethe.*

DOUBT—It is impossible for that man to despair who remembers that his Helper is omnipotent.—*Jeremy Taylor.*

TIGHTENED CORDS—Failure will hurt but not hinder us. Disillusion will pain but not dishearten us. Sorrows will shake us but not break us. Hope will set the music ringing and quicken our lagging pace. We need hope for living far more than for dying. Dying is easy work compared with living. Dying is a moment's transition; living, a transaction of years. It is the length of the rope that puts the sag in it. Hope tightens the cords and tunes up the heart-strings. Work well, then; suffer patiently, rejoicing in hope. God knows all, and yet is the God of Hope. And when we have hoped to the end here, He will give us something to look forward to, for all eternity. For "hope abideth."—*Babcock.*

Foolish Pride

When I complained that I had lost my
    hope
Of life eternal with eternal God;
When I refused to read my horoscope
In the unchanging stars, or claim abode
With powers and dominations—but, poor
    clod,
Clung to the earth and grovelled in my
    tears,
Because I soon must lie beneath the sod
And close the little number of my years,—
Then I was told that pride had barred the
    way
And raised this foul rebellion in my head.
Yet, strange rebellion! I, but yesterday,
Was God's own son in His own likeness
    bred.
And thrice strange pride! who thus am
    cast away
And go forth lost and disinherited.
    —*Wilfred Scawen Blunt.*

LOYALTY — There is related in the book, "The Czar," a story of a Russian officer taken prisoner by the French. They got an iron and branded him on the hand with an "N." When he asked what it meant, they said, "It means that you belong, body and soul, to the Emperor Napoleon." The soldier, seizing an axe, severed his hand from the wrist and said, "Take what belongs to you; I am for the Czar, and belong to him." Whether fact or fiction, it shows what entire consecration means, and the kind of loyalty, whole-souled loyalty, Jesus claims for Himself.

—*Chapman.*

HOLDING

In the bitter waves of woe,
  Beaten and tossed about
By the sullen winds that blow
  From the desolate shores of doubt,
Where the anchors that faith has cast
  Are dragging in the gale,
I am quietly holding fast
  To the things that cannot fail.

—*Washington Gladden.*

LIMITATIONS — A child might say to a geographer, "You talk about the earth being round! Look on this great crag; look on that deep dell; look on yonder great mountain, and the valley at its feet, and yet you talk about the earth being round." The geographer would have an instant answer for the child. His view is comprehensive; he does not look at the surface of the world in mere detail; he does not deal with inches, and feet, and yards; he sees a larger world than the child has had time to grasp. He explains what he means by the expression, "The earth is a globe," and justifies his strange statement. And so it is with God's wonderful dealings towards us; there are great rocks and barren deserts, deep, dank, dark pits, and defiles, and glens, and dells, rugged places that we cannot smooth over at all, and yet when He comes to say to us at the end of the journey, "Now look back; there is the way that I have brought you," we shall be enabled to say, "Thou has gone before us and made our way straight."—*Joseph Parker.*

CONVICTION—A man without convictions is a tramp on the road that leads to the land of nowhere.—*Evangelist.*

TRANSCENDENT — We do not have to go to the universe to prove the existence of God from design. We do not have to dig down into the bowels of the earth, nor go up to the stars for proofs of the divine existence. He is not far from every one of us. As Paul says, "In Him we move and have our being;" and as Tennyson says, "Closer is He than breathing; and nearer than hands and feet." God is here. There is no escaping Him. Man is under moral law as well as physical, and if he violates the one code or the other, the penalty will in each case be inflicted. I put my hand in the fire and feel physical pain; that is proof that I have a physical system. I perform a bad action and feel the sting of conscience and the pangs of remorse; that is equally a proof that I have a moral nature. Who made the act?—I did. Who made the pain?—Some one not myself, whom I call God.—*Parkhurst.*

It fortifies my soul to know
That though I perish, truth is so;
That, howso'er I stray and range,
Whate'er I do, Thou dost not change.
I steadier step when I recall
That, if I slip, Thou dost not fall.

—*Arthur Hugh Clough.*

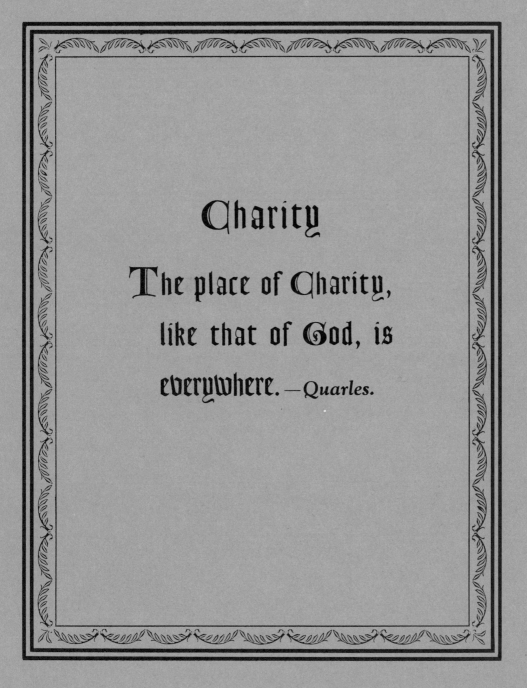

Charity

The place of Charity,
like that of God, is
everywhere. —Quarles.